EIR (ISSN 0273-6314) *is published weekly
(50 issues), by EIR News Service, Inc.,
P.O. Box 17390, Washington, D.C. 20041-0390.
(703) 777-9451*

European Headquarters: E.I.R. GmbH, Postfach
Bahnstrasse 9a, D-65205, Wiesbaden, Germany
Tel: 49-611-73650
Homepage: http://www.eirna.com
e-mail: eirna@eirna.com
Director: Georg Neudecker

Montreal, Canada: 514-461-1557

Denmark: EIR - Danmark, Sankt Knuds Vej 11,
basement left, DK-1903 Frederiksberg, Denmark.
Tel.: +45 35 43 60 40, Fax: +45 35 43 87 57. e-mail:
eirdk@hotmail.com.

Mexico City: EIR, Sor Juana Inés de la Cruz 242-2
Col. Agricultura C.P. 11360
Delegación M. Hidalgo, México D.F.
Tel. (5525) 5318-2301
eirmexico@gmail.com

New Opportunities For Mankind

This is a Revolution

by Lyndon LaRouche, Jr.

From some remarks by LaRouche to the LaRouche PAC Policy Committee on September 28, 2015

Sept. 28—I can say that the developments of this past week, and coming on still, are really exemplary of something. We're not quite sure what they're exemplary of, but we do know that it involves Putin. And Putin is actually the keystone, right now,—he's the keystone of the future of mankind, and in his operation, the future's going to be there. China, of course, is a big factor in this, and some other people, known to me personally, are also key people in this operation. And that will be a little bit of a surprise to most people, because we'll hold that back for a couple of weeks, or a week or so.

So, therefore, we are actually in a unique situation. We are placed in the right place. Our numerically small organization has suddenly become very large, in many implications, including the fun department, the musical fun department, and things like that,—which is what has to go with a thing like this. And we have a lot of fun with Manhattan, and Manhattan, of course, is the place where the creation of our organization started.

I think there will be some more eventful developments coming out very soon. Of course, the destiny of Obama is also among the mysteries which have to be resolved now, because this is a change. It's a fundamental change in policy. And, actually, we as ourselves (because most people don't know what has happened here); we, a smaller group of people, know internationally, as well as in the United States,—this group that we

UN/Cia Pak

Russian President Putin at the UN Sept. 28: "We can no longer tolerate the current state of affairs in the world."

represent, has a lot of knowledge about these matters, and I can assure you that there will be much more attention to those relationships very soon.

We have some responsibilities now in this matter. There are some things I won't mention, which are important things, but they're not ready to be mentioned, shall we say. But more is going to be brought forth more clearly when I present that,—which will be later. This is a revolution. There's a matter of risk in it; there are elements of risk in it. *But!* If you look at the thing the way I see it, from my personal viewpoint, we're on the edge of something *very, very big,* and *very, very important* for all of mankind. This is an opening, the like of which has never occurred before. So begin to enjoy it.

The U.S.A. Is Not Just a Nation

Well, the one thing you want to put together because of the nature of these events in the United States right now, is that the United States is not just a nation. There is something *inside* the United States which is much more than merely a nation, and very few Americans so far have actually understood that. First of all the creation of the United States had its roots in the Renaissance, and you've got to go back to the Renaissance in order to locate the origins of the United States. Nicholas of Cusa was *merely,*—to say the word "*merely,*"—was actually a part of a process which developed, and which Nicholas of Cusa actually began to express in his own way, and reinforce this achievement. But the *concept* had already existed!

And it was from the genesis of that origin that the birth of the United States as a possibility came into existence. But you have to go through the history of these people, like Kepler and others, who played a key role in this process. This focussed on the need for a new kind of society against the European system, against other parts of the world system, and said, "This instrument of a government *is necessary for all mankind*." And there is a quality inside the United States, built into it, often not recognized or identified by the average American, for example,—but it exists. And if you understand the history, as I've had a passionate insight into what history really means,—No, this is real history.

And therefore, what follows from that is not the effects of what Americans have done, as such; it's the question of what has been done on their behalf, by what would be for most people, a mysterious source. Because that's what the United States really must represent, even though the behavior of Americans is not really very intelligent for most of the time. But inside the creation of the United States,—as from Kepler, for example, what's Kepler? Kepler's just a scientist? No! He's not! He's one of the persons who defined what the Solar System means! He defined the meaning of the Solar System; he defined the meaning of the relationship of mankind to other parts of the universe.

And it was this kind of thing, the roots of this, which made the existence of the United States possible. It would not have meant anything otherwise, except in that way. And we have to understand that.

And therefore, we're assembling in Manhattan and around there. What does that mean? Well, most people don't know anything about it. They feel the presence of it, but they don't know the meaning of it. And what I've been seeing in this period is this sense of the justification of the existence of the United States, which most

UN/Cia Pak

Chinese President Xi Jinping, in his toast at his State Dinner with President Obama Sept. 26, said: "As an ancient Chinese saying goes: 'Only those who take actions can achieve their goal. Only those who strive forward can reach their destination.' President Abraham Lincoln once said: 'The best way to predict the future is to create it.'" Xi is shown here at the UN summit on development Sept. 26, 2015.

Americans don't understand. But I think the time has come, that we ought to give them a little more information about this great mystery of the creation of the United States.

What's the Meaning of Mankind?

I say this repeatedly, but the question is: what's the meaning of mankind? And the meaning of mankind is the creative powers of mankind. And it's unique, because mankind is the only living species we know of who has this ability, who has this quality,—the creative powers of the human mind. But the important thing which is often lost, is what's the mystery? Well, the mystery is that people die, yes. But that's not the point. They also have progeny, or they develop progeny, and the progeny improve,—or the intention is that the progeny must improve,—as the United States in its own funny way progressed, and brought an effect on the planet as a whole, which improved the planet as a whole, or created the roots for that.

People lose that because they don't identify it; and I've been emphasizing repeatedly that *you've got to look at that point*. If you want to understand this, you've got to say, "What is the meaning of human life, as opposed to anything *except* human life?" And that is that mankind is a creative force. A creative force which changes the universe, and will change the universe; and therefore, we in the United States have captured an aspect of that destiny of man, as a creative force within the Solar System, and more.

And that's what we should be celebrating. We should be bringing our own people more and more into an understanding of the meaning of life. Because you have to take the meaning of life and say, "It's not the meaning of *death*." It's something that goes with death, but also it means the progress of mankind in the process of death; death grows. But in the right process, mankind

Gregory F. Maxwell

The immortal Abraham Lincoln, as depicted in the Lincoln Memorial in Washington, D.C.

is developing. Because in each generation that is progressive, relative to the older generations, there's a process that's going on. And the process is what we call "human creativity."

And this is the time,—in the circumstances of these days, presently,—this is the time to think in those terms.

Mankind's Mission

The only thing that's important about mankind, is what mankind is uniquely capable of doing in terms of our knowledge of the Solar System and beyond. That's the mission. It's not some ambition or something, but the idea is that each generation of mankind *should*, if at all possible, progress to a higher level of productivity, of intellectual productivity, creativity,—and that's the purpose of mankind.

And what we see as evil, is nothing but just that: Wall Street, for example, is evil; it's intrinsically evil. It always was intrinsically evil. Why? Because it's a completely destructive force. It's chewing up things, destroying things, eating things, destroying planets, destroying people!

And we've now come to a very interesting period of life, and of our history: We have a global development which is gripping us now. We have not caught up with it, but it will grip us, as it's gripping us now.

Obama and his Stepfather

I think there's one thing that we do have a record of as an organization: We do know what the relationship is of Obama, President Obama, and his stepfather. The history is well-known, including the history of the mother's role in this operation. The sobriquets and so forth of the experience of the father, and the son and mother; the mother was of the least importance there; the father was an ogre, a real ogre, a man-eater, a destroyer, a killer. And Obama was trained by his stepfather. And the stepfather produced a monster, a criminal in the extreme, a man whose very existence is criminality, is the expression of criminality and nothing else. He is *pure evil* and nothing else!

And because of his influence, he's a big evil which must be removed from society. Remove him from power; put him into obloquy. Just get rid of him, put him out of the way. Put him in a corner some place, let him rot in his own way.

And the problem is that the people of the United States, too many of them, have capitulated to losing their own soul by supporting Obama. Any American who supports Obama has lost his soul, guaranteed!

And this is the issue: that we have a Satanic force, which has a very important role in terms of the planet as a whole,—it's called "Obama." Obama is really nothing except a *force of evil*. He was trained in evil by his stepfather, and that's the history of the thing! And if you don't see Obama in that, if you see Obama as containing something different than that, then you're a fool! Because this man is Satanic. And he's expressed this in every possible way, a Satanic force. And that's what we're up against.

But the planet somehow, the world in general, seems to be in a mood to get rid of this force of evil. We're going to see what happens this week. The thing is live now,—this man is going to show his Satanic characteristics very soon this week.

EIR Contents

www.larouchepub.com Volume 42, Number 39, October 2, 2015

NASA

Cover This Week

An image of spiral galaxy NGC 3521 from the NASA/ESA Hubble Space telescope.

The End of the Imperial Money System

by Robert Ingraham

Sept. 26—*Things were not always as they now are.* The current fashionable axioms of the Twenty-First Century trans-Atlantic community, now blindly obeyed and unchallenged by the vast majority of that region's population, are not in fact either self-evident truths or products of rigorous scientific investigation. The axioms and commonly held beliefs of today, which cover every aspect of human life from economics, to music and to science, are just that—unsupported, unexamined, and groundless "belief structures" which have been imposed on human culture beginning with the British empiricist onslaught, led by Bertrand Russell, at the beginning of the Twentieth Century.

For the United States, September 14, 1901 was the turning point. Prior to that fateful day, for forty years, the successive Presidencies of Abraham Lincoln, Ulysses Grant, and William McKinley, had succeeded in returning the American Republic to the original intent of the Washington Presidency, and that Administration's philosophical outlook

Library of Congress
President William McKinley gives his Inaugural Address on March 4, 1897.

as embodied in the Constitutional Principle of Alexander Hamilton.

Throughout the history of American culture, there is a coherent philosophical and economic outlook which stretches from Lincoln through Grant to McKinley. On April 6, 1858, Abraham Lincoln delivered a lecture at Bloomington, Illinois titled "Discoveries and Inventions." That lecture both encapsulates Lincoln's views on economic policy as well as his insight into the creative identity of the human species, while at the same time the philosophical outlook of that lecture is fully coherent with the Principle of republican Human Development as identified by Alexander Hamilton in his Reports of 1790-1791. That Lincoln enunciation on human creativity and economic development—as policy intent—was carried forward by the Presidencies of Grant and McKinley and was only terminated by the bullet of a British-deployed assassin.

We are dealing with axioms of policy here, not reforms of existing structures within the currently accepted axioms. For example:

Current financial policies of the Federal Reserve and the U.S. Treasury have routinely been attacked from both the "left" and the "right." The 2011 "Occupy Wall Street" phenomenon protested Wall Street "abuses" and the inequality of incomes and living standards within the United States. Similarly, on the "right," after 2007, many "Tea Party" groups denounced the Wall Street "bailouts," and of course, for the truly esoteric, there exists the John Birch/Eustace Mullins exposés of the Federal Reserve, Jekyll Island and the "Money Trust." What all of these protests, whether from the left or right, have in common is that they merely focus on "abuses" of the financial system, or on who "controls" the financial system. Whether well-meaning or not, all of these protesters err by accepting the axiomatic existence of that Money System itself. But this Money System is not self-evident; nor has it existed forever, as a feature of human culture.

What we are discussing here is the CREATION of the Money System, an alien parasite brought into our nation after the murder of a U.S. President, and a system now accepted after more than 100 years as self-evident. That imperial monetarist system were better named the *Bertrand Russell Monetary System*, because its creation and its axioms all derive from the mathematical empiricism of Russell, and both the underlying axioms and the day-to-day practice of that system all deny—as Russell himself does—the actual creative nature of the human species.

I. Hamilton—and Human Economics

The philosophical content of *Hamilton's Principle* has been identified and discussed at length by Lyndon LaRouche in many locations. The political and strategic nature of Hamilton's efforts has been presented by this author in an earlier article published in the *Executive Intelligence Review*.[1] For our present purposes it is enough to state that for Hamilton, the intention of the Constitutional Republic was to engender an ever-increasing increase in the productivity of the nation.

This should not be understood from a mere accounting standpoint, i.e., as an increase in monetary profit margins for the nation's enterprises, but rather a continuous increase in the productive power of the workforce, through a deliberate fostering of scientific, technological, and industrial revolutions which increase mankind's "power over nature." It should also be stressed that such an approach commits the nation to

---

1. See *Manhattan's Struggle Against the Slave Power of Virginia*, available here.

Hamiltonian Credit

American economist Lyndon LaRouche spelled out "Alexander Hamilton's credit principle" succinctly in a Jan. 22, 2011 webcast:

"Honest debt to the future can be paid only through honest creation of future physical and equivalent wealth, including the development of the relevant creative powers of the individual citizen, and also the children and adolescents of those families.

"Such debts of a credit system must be paid by the fruitfulness of future production, as this principle was already understood by the Winthrops and Mathers of the original Massachusetts colony. Such debts require that the government delimit such accumulations of debt to the efficient commitment to promote that production. Such debt can be lawfully incurred only by a decision premised on a reasonable expectation of the relevant creation of the increased physical wealth, and of the increased physical productivity of the nation. Debts incurred on the account of financial speculation are not legitimate debts of a government.

"This describes, in rather plain language, Alexander Hamilton's great principle, as embedded in the subsuming intent of the Preamble of our Federal Constitution. Debts are good, when they are designed to be made good, as by a credit system based on a commitment to increase the creation of net wealth per capita, and per square kilometer of the territory of a nation."

the fostering of not only an increase in living standards, but a deliberate policy of improving the cognitive and cultural abilities—power—of the nation's citizenry. In essence, this is a future-oriented policy orientation, i.e., actual Value lies not in the dollar-denominated workings of the current market-place, but rather in the creation of a future, as-yet-unrealized, higher order of existence.

Much could be said about the specifics of Hamilton's economic program, but it is the *intent*, as it flowed from both his understanding of the creative nature of the human species, as well as from the proper role of government in fostering such positive developments, which is the key to the matter.

In truth, economics, properly defined, has nothing to do with money. Economics is actually the study of people, or, more precisely, the study of the physical and cognitive progress of the human species. The use of Fire was discovered by mankind more than one million years ago. Pre-historic discoveries in the fields of astronomy, navigation, and metallurgy all dramatically helped to transform man's relationship with the world around him and led to the expansion and uplifting of the species. This is Human Progress, something no beast is capable of, and it is made possible by creative human discoveries, not by money, nor by the mere buying and selling of goods as defined by Adam Smith.

Hamilton developed not a monetary system, but rather a sovereign national credit system through which the necessary physical economic development and the concomitant increase in the cognitive power of the citizenry could be supported and advanced, a development actually coherent with our species nature. That is the principle upon which the nation was created between 1787 and 1797. This is not mere assertion. A careful reading of, for example, Hamilton's *Report on Manufactures* demonstrates that any contrary interpretation of the intent of the first Washington Administration is incompetent.

Economics is not value-less, nor amoral; it is grounded in the advancement of the species, the love of the species, the celebration of those qualities which separate us from the beasts. Only human beings are capable of conceptualizing current policy based on a future orientation, a future development of the power of the species. That truth is what Hamilton and his friends fought for, and that is what was lost in 1901.

II. From Lincoln to McKinley

On April 27, 1893 William McKinley delivered a eulogy for Ulysses S. Grant at Galena, Illinois on the seventy-first anniversary of Grant's birth. Less than two years later, on February 12, 1895 McKinley delivered a eulogy in Albany, New York for Abraham Lincoln on the eighty-sixth anniversary of his birth.

The most striking thing about these two eulogies is the continuity of philosophical outlook. In the Eulogy for Lincoln, McKinley says:

> The greatest names in American history are Washington and Lincoln. One is forever associated with the independence of the States and formation of the Federal Union; the other with universal freedom and the preservation of the Union. Washington enforced the Declaration of Independence as against England; Lincoln proclaimed its fulfillment not only to a downtrodden race in America, but to all people for all time who may seek the protection of our flag. These illustrious men achieved grander results for mankind within a single century, from 1775 to 1865, than any other men ever accomplished in all the years since first the flight of time began....
>
> The present generation knows Washington only from history, and by that alone can judge him. Lincoln we know by history also, but thousands are still living who participated in the great events in which he was leader and master. Many of his contemporaries survived him; some are here yet in almost every locality. So Lincoln is not far removed from us; he may be said to be still known to the millions—not surrounded by the mist of antiquity, nor a halo of idolatry that is impenetrable.

And in the Eulogy for Grant, he states:

> With no disparagement to others, two names rise above all the rest in American history since George Washington—transcendently above them. They are Abraham Lincoln and Ulysses S. Grant. Each will be remembered for what he did and accomplished for his race and for mankind. Lincoln proclaimed liberty

President McKinley speaks at the 40th anniversary of the Lincoln-Douglas debate in Galesburg, Illinois, in October 1898.

to four million slaves, and upon his act invited "the considerate judgment of mankind and the gracious favor of Almighty God." He has received the warm approval of the one, and I am sure he is enjoying the generous benediction of the other.

His was the greatest, mightiest stroke of the war. Grand on its humanity side, masterly in its military aspect, it has given to his name an imperishable place among men. Grant gave irresistible power and efficacy to the Proclamation of Liberty. The iron shackles which Lincoln declared should be loosed from the limbs and souls of the black slaves, Grant with his matchless army melted and destroyed in the burning glories of the war; and the rebels read the inspired decree in the flashing guns of his artillery, and they knew what Lincoln had decreed Grant would execute . . . . Grant believed in the brotherhood of man—in the political equality of all men—he had secured that with his sword, and was prompt to recognize it in all places and everywhere. . . .

We are not a Nation of hero worshipers. We are a Nation of generous freemen. We bow in affectionate reverence and with most grateful

hearts to these immortal names, Washington, Lincoln, and Grant, and will guard with sleepless vigilance their mighty work and cherish their memories evermore.

These two short eulogies provide the key to understanding McKinley the man, as well as the initiatives of his Presidency. For McKinley, the promise and the intent of the Washington, Lincoln, and Grant Presidencies represented a living vital commitment on his part to continue their work to further the principles of the American Revolution. Nothing about the McKinley Presidency can be understood unless one begins with that underlying truth.

Defending Black Equality

In the context of the brief overview provided in this article, there are two aspects to this personal commitment of McKinley's worth discussing here.

The first of these, either rarely mentioned or downplayed in most biographies of McKinley, was McKinley's moral determination to continue the efforts of Lincoln and Grant on behalf of Black Americans in the South. By the 1890s this was a very difficult proposition. After the withdrawal of Federal troops from the South by President Hayes in 1877, the unrepentant forces of the Confederacy began to reassert control in state after state. In 1872 full amnesty was granted to almost all of the leaders of the former Confederate States of America and those white-supremacists subsequently returned to elected offices both in state governments and in the U.S. Congress itself. By 1877 all of the states in the South, except South Carolina, Florida, and Louisiana had reverted to white rule. In 1890 the arch-racist Benjamin Tillman responded to his election as Governor of South Carolina by saying, "The triumph of Democracy and white supremacy over mongrelism and anarchy is most complete."

Also in 1890 the state of Mississippi repudiated its "Reconstruction Constitution," one which guaranteed equal rights for blacks, and adopted a new constitution which removed blacks from elected office and denied them the right to vote. Almost every state in the South soon followed Mississippi's example. Then, in 1896—

Library of Congress

The crowd gathered outside William McKinley's house during his 1896 "front porch" campaign for President, reflects his broad constituency.

the very year that McKinley was elected President—the Supreme Court handed down the *Plessy v. Ferguson* decision, effectively nullifying the intent of the Fourteenth and Fifteenth Amendments, and imposing on the entire nation the racial philosophy of the Southern Confederates.

During those years a split developed within the Republican Party in the South, and two competing organizations emerged. These became known as the *Black-and-Tan Republicans*, an integrated alliance committed to a continuation of the Lincoln/Grant policy, including the policy of full voting rights for southern blacks, and the *Lily-White Republicans*, who acquiesced to Jim Crow rule, and who, by the 1880s, began purging black officials from their ranks.

Beginning with his years in Congress, and continuing through his Presidency, McKinley allied with the

Black-and-Tans, and it was southern Black-and-Tan delegates who played a critical role in securing the Presidential nomination for McKinley at the 1896 Republican Convention.[2] From 1877 through 1901 there was probably no other national figure in the Republican Party who fought harder against the resurgence of the Confederacy than McKinley. During his first term, McKinley did what he could to aid the former southern black Congressmen who had lost their positions as Jim Crow took control. These included Blanche Kelso Bruce, Robert Smalls, John Roy Lynch, Henry Plummer Cheatham, and Thomas Ezekiel Miller.

He also spoke out against Southern lynchings,[3] supported the rights of the Black U.S. Army regiments (the "Buffalo Soldiers"), and used his power of federal appointment to secure non-elective positions, such as Postmasters, for many southern black Republicans.

Shortly after the Civil War, in 1867, McKinley had delivered his first-ever public speech. It was titled "On Black Equality." An excerpt follows:

My friends and fellow-citizens, the settlements of that war—and I speak for my comrades of the Grand Army of the Republic—the settlements of that war must stand as the irreversible judgment of battle and the inflexible decree of a Nation of free men. They must not be misinterpreted, they must not be nullified, they must not be weakened or shorn of their force under any pretext whatsoever.... It must not be equality and justice in the written law only. It must be equality and justice in the law's administration everywhere, and alike administered in every part of the Republic to every citizen thereof. It must not be the cold formality of constitutional enactment. It must be a living birthright....

Our black allies must neither be forsaken nor

---

2. Conversely, in both 1904 and 1912 it would be the Lily-White Republicans who would mobilize on behalf of Teddy Roosevelt.

3. By the 1890s there were over 200 lynchings per year in the South.

deserted. I weigh my words. This is the great question not only of the present, but is the great question of the future; and this question will never be settled until it is settled upon principles of justice, recognizing the sanctity of the Constitution of the United States. We cherish no resentments from the war; we have no bitterness against the people of the South. We want them to be our brothers, not only in name but in spirit and heart. We bid them enjoy equally our prosperity. But at the same time we bid them obey the Constitution of the country.... Nothing can be permanently settled until the right of every citizen to participate equally in our State and National affairs is unalterably

Brevet Major William McKinley during the Civil War. He was the last Civil War veteran to become President of the United States.

fixed. Tariff, finance, civil service, and all other political and party questions should remain open and unsettled until every citizen who has a constitutional right to share in the determination is free to enjoy it.

McKinley never wavered from that outlook. It should also be noted that, following the Civil War, in a legal career which lasted from 1867 to 1876, McKinley became famous for defending the rights of labor unions and working men. In one of his most celebrated cases, McKinley defended a group of coal miners arrested for rioting after a clash with strikebreakers. McKinley took the case *pro bono* (without pay) against the opposing group of mine owners. He was successful in obtaining acquittals for all but one of the defendants.

Grand Army of the Republic

William McKinley was the last Civil War veteran to serve in the White House. He had joined the 23rd Ohio Infantry in 1861, rising from Private to Major by the war's end. During most of 1864 and 1865 the Ohio 23rd served under the overall command of General Philip Sheridan, during his campaigns in the Shenandoah Valley. It was this military service, and the mission of the Union Army, under the command of Ulysses Grant, which defines a second axiomatic feature of the entirety

of McKinley's later career. His continuing loyalty, his faithfulness, in honoring the mission and the sacrifices of the Union Army were afterwards always present in the motivations of his life's mission.

As years passed, one of the critical conduits in linking his Civil War service and the Grant Presidency to his own later Presidency was McKinley's relationship with the MacArthur family. Douglas MacArthur's grandfather, Arthur MacArthur Sr., had been a close friend and ally of Ulysses Grant, and when Grant returned from his World Tour in 1879, he visited MacArthur and discussed with him the significance of, in particular, his meetings with the leaders of China and Japan. Four years later, in 1883, MacArthur's son, Arthur MacArthur Jr., authored a paper titled "China Memorandum and Notes," which his father presented to Ulysses Grant in a bid by Arthur to become America's first military attaché to China. In that paper Arthur Jr. argued for an American commitment to defend the nations of east Asia against the designs of the British Empire.[4]

Later, after the Spanish-American War, Arthur MacArthur Jr. would not only be named Military Governor of the Philippines by President McKinley, but in 1905-1906 he would follow in the footsteps of Ulysses Grant with a tour of Asia that included visits to Japan, Shanghai, Hong Kong, Ceylon, a trip across India, Burma, Bangkok, Singapore, Rangoon, and Saigon. He was accompanied on this tour by his son Douglas MacArthur. Only five days before his assassination, McKinley met with Arthur MacArthur at McKinley's home in Canton, Ohio. This McKinley/MacArthur discussion, of which there is no record, occurred precisely at the moment that McKinley was moving to put into place new policies and new relationships in both Asia and Latin America in opposition to the British Empire.

---

4. Arthur MacArthur Jr., as is well-known, was also the 18 year-old hero of the 1863 Battle of Missionary Ridge, where troops under the command of Ulysses Grant, William Tecumseh Sherman and Philip Sheridan broke the back of the Confederate Army of Tennessee.

III. A Community of Republican Principle Among Nations

The primary identity that most amateur historians aver about William McKinley is that he was the "Champion of Protectionism." However, labeling McKinley as simply a supporter of high protective tariffs, is not only extremely simplistic, but, more importantly, actually wrong as to McKinley's motives and intent. McKinley was an *anti-imperial peace-builder.* It was neither narrow nationalism, nor simplistic "protectionism" which motivated his actions.

Beginning as early as his years in Congress, and becoming a central feature of his Presidency, McKinley increasingly put forward a policy then known by the name of *"Reciprocity,"* a policy also closely associated with Maine Republican leader and statesman James Blaine. Under McKinley this idea of Reciprocity became the guidepost for all of U.S. foreign policy, particularly toward the nations of Latin America. As the word implies, this was a policy of partnership among nations, particularly in the areas of mutually beneficial economic, scientific, and industrial development.

Two views of the 1901 Buffalo, New York Pan-American Exposition, the organization of which reflected McKinley's commitment to international cooperation for technological progress.

The day before his assassination, William McKinley delivered his final speech, one which contains his mature views which were intended to guide his second term as President. The speech was delivered at the Pan-American Exposition, in Buffalo, Sept. 5, 1901. Excerpts follow:

Expositions are the timekeepers of progress. They record the world's advancement. They stimulate the energy, enterprise, and intellect of the people, and quicken human genius. They go into the home. They broaden and brighten the daily life of the people. They open mighty storehouses of information to the student. Every exposition, great or small, has helped to some onward step....

The Pan-American Exposition has done its work thoroughly, presenting in its exhibits evidences of the highest skill and illustrating the progress of the human family in the western hemisphere. This portion of the earth has no cause for humiliation for the part it has performed in the march of civilization. It has not accomplished everything; far from it. It has simply done its best, and without vanity or boastfulness and recognizing the manifold achievements of others, it invites the friendly rivalry of all the powers in the peaceful pursuits of trade and commerce, and will co-operate with all in advancing the highest and best interests of humanity....

The wisdom and energy of all the nations are none too great for the world's work. The success of art, science, industry, and invention is an international asset and a common glory. After all, how near one to the other is every part of the world. Modern inventions have brought into close relation widely separated peoples, and made them better acquainted. Geographic and political divisions will continue to exist, but distances have been effaced.

The period of exclusiveness is past. The expansion of our trade and commerce is the pressing problem. Commercial wars are unprofitable. A policy of good will and friendly trade relations will prevent reprisals.

Reciprocity treaties are in harmony with the spirit of the times; measures of retaliation are not. If, perchance, some of our tariffs are no longer needed for revenue or to encourage and protect our industries at home, why should they not be employed to extend and promote our markets abroad? Then, too, we have inadequate steamship service. New lines of steamships have already been put in commission between the Pacific coast ports of the United States and those on the western coasts of Mexico and Central and South America. These should be followed up with direct steamship lines between the western coast of the United States and South American ports. One of the needs of the times is direct commercial lines from our vast fields of production to the fields of consumption that we have but barely touched.

We must build the Isthmian Canal, which will unite the two oceans and give a straight line of water communication with the western coasts of Central and South America and Mexico. The construction of a Pacific cable cannot be longer postponed. In the furtherance of these objects of national interest and concern you are performing an important part. This Exposition would have touched the heart of that American statesman whose mind was ever alert and thought ever constant for a larger commerce and a truer fraternity of the republics of the New World. His broad American spirit is felt and manifested here. He

Library of Congress

Excavation of the Panama Canal in 1907. This was one of the development projects for the Americas which President McKinley envisioned carrying out in cooperation with the nations of South America.

needs no identification to an assemblage of Americans anywhere, for the name of Blaine is inseparably associated with the Pan-American movement which finds here practical and substantial expression, and which we all hope will be firmly advanced by the Pan-American Congress that assembles this Autumn in the capital of Mexico.

The good work will go on. It cannot be stopped. These buildings will disappear, this creation of art and beauty and industry will perish from sight, but their influence will remain to "Make it live beyond its too short living with praises and thanksgiving."

Gentlemen, let us ever remember that our interest is in concord, not conflict, and that our real eminence rests in the victories of peace, not those of war. We hope that all who are represented here may be moved to higher and nobler effort for their own and the world's good, and that out of this city may come not only greater commerce and trade for us all, but, more essential than these, relations of mutual respect, confidence, and friendship, which will deepen and endure.

Our earnest prayer is that God will graciously vouchsafe prosperity, happiness, and peace to all our neighbors and like blessings to all the peoples and powers of earth.

Some Brief Remarks on Historical Background

Space constraints do not allow a full exposition of all of the events surrounding the McKinley Presidency. The following will have to suffice.

On the Spanish-American War: McKinley strongly opposed the Spanish-American War and did everything he could to prevent its outbreak, even after the destruction of the USS Maine. Once the war began, his overriding concern was that it not be turned into an imperial war.

McKinley recognized that the cause of the Cuban rebels was just, that the Cuban rebellion basically pitted former black slaves and native Indians against the atrocities of the colonial Spanish, and he was deliberate in his approach that we were aiding the natives of Cuba to free themselves from colonialism. As for the Philippines, although it was a more difficult situation than Cuba, once again, both McKinley and Arthur Mac-Arthur viewed their mission as one of spreading republicanism and economic development into Asia. This view of justice for Asians also extended to McKinley's intervention into the Chinese Boxer Rebellion, where he acted independent of the European powers to thwart British designs on China and to defend the sovereignty of that nation.

The McKinley Administration also cooperated with Russia on the development of the trans-Siberian Railroad, including by sending Ethan Allan Hitchcock as Ambassador to Russia where he worked closely with Count Sergei Witte on the project.

McKinley's actions in the Philippines, China, and

Library of Congress

McKinley's ambassador to Russia, Gen. Ethan A. Hitchcock, was tasked with collaborating with the Russian government in great projects such as the trans-Siberian railroad. He served in 1897.

Russia were not individual initiatives. It is clear that by 1900 McKinley believed that the United States was powerful enough and possessed sufficient economic might—for the first time in its history—to step onto the world stage as a direct challenger to the hegemony of the British Empire. The policy of Reciprocity, for example, represented the vision of a new republican world order, a mortal danger to British imperialism. It is also clear that McKinley (as well as Arthur MacArthur) viewed east Asia as the primary battleground against the British.

McKinley is generally portrayed as a strong opponent of "soft money," and it is true he battled the incompetent "silver crusade" of William Jennings Bryan, which would have saddled the United States with an artificial, wildly inflated currency. However, during his first term McKinley made strenuous efforts to recruit other nations into a "bimetallic," i.e, silver and gold, global monetary standard. France and several other nations agreed to the convening of an international conference on bimetallism, but British sabotage prevented that conference from ever taking place.

It was also McKinley who led the nation back to economic recovery from the deep depression of 1892-1897. The banking Panic of 1893 was followed by the closure of more than 500 banks and by tens of thousands of business failures. National unemployment rose from 3 million in 1892 to 15 million in 1896. President Grover Cleveland unsuccessfully tried to stem the collapse with gold purchases from Wall Street and other financial manipulations, but it was the election of McKinley and his actions to stabilize trade and production which turned the tide. One action taken by McKinley was the expansion of the number of National Banks with small capital, to protect farmers and other western interests from credit starvation.

While serving in Congress, later as Governor of Ohio, and finally as President, McKinley stood forthright as a champion of the "General Welfare," including

McKinley's election poster reflects his campaign for the "general welfare" and international cooperation.

as a defender of the rights and living standards of trade unions and working people. One example of this was his sponsorship of federal legislation mandating an eight-hour work day for all federal employees. The late Nineteenth Century was a period of continual social convulsions, largely arising from London-created "Panics" which repeatedly plunged the United States into economic crisis and mass unemployment. Violence, labor unrest, and strikes were the inevitable consequences of these crises. Throughout those years, McKinley repeatedly acted to defend working Americans, including during the famous "Debs Rebellion" (national railroad strike) of 1894.

1901—the Turning Point

On March 13, 1881, the great reformer and the defender of the United States from 1862 to 1865, the Czar of Russia Alexander II, was assassinated. Nine years later the pro-American German Chancellor Otto von Bismarck was removed from office in a political *coup d'état*. Both men had held extensive discussions with Ulysses Grant during his 1878-1879 World Tour, and both were in complete concord with the policy orientation of the Lincoln and Grant Presidencies. They were America's two most important partners on the world stage.

Then, between 1894 and 1900, the President of France Sadi Carnot (1894), the Spanish Premier (1897), the Empress of Austria (1898), and the King of Italy (1900) were all assassinated, almost all of them by British-steered anarchists. This was all part of the British build-up toward World War I.

Then, on September 6, 1901, President William McKinley, the last Lincoln Republican to occupy the White House, was shot twice at the Pan-American Exposition in Buffalo, New York by Leon Czolgosz, a protégé of the Russian-American anarchist Emma Goldman.[5] Eight days later McKinley died from his wounds.

Teddy Roosevelt, stepping into office over the bloody body of McKinley, then proceeded to reverse every one of McKinley's policies. Reciprocity and friendship with foreign nations, and the promulgation of American republican ideals were replaced by the policy of the "Big Stick" and colonialism. Britain became our dearest ally. The westward Manifest Destiny of American development was halted as Roosevelt launched the modern environmentalist movement and proceeded to lock up western lands. The blacks of the South were utterly abandoned as Roosevelt allied himself with the Lily-Whites and turned a blind eye to lynchings and mass murder.

In 1908 Roosevelt established the Bureau of Investigation (BOI), the forerunner of today's FBI. When Congress refused to allocate funds for what they charged was a nationwide "secret police," Roosevelt instructed Attorney General Charles Bonaparte to establish the agency under Presidential authority.

Two years later, following the wrenching financial

---

5. Czolgosz had met with Goldman, an advocate of political assassination, at her home in Cleveland in June 1901, and, during Czolgosz's subsequent trial, Goldman authored an article titled *"The Tragedy at Buffalo,"* wherein she defended Czolgosz's killing of McKinley and compared it to the assassination of Julius Caesar by Marcus Junius Brutus.

Panic of 1907,[6] Roosevelt led the way in establishing the National Monetary Commission, a group charged with "reforming" America's banking and financial system. It was the work of that Commission which led directly to the infamous 1910 Jekyll Island tryst, whose end product was the establishment of the U.S. Federal Reserve in 1913.

By 1915 the Lincoln-Grant-McKinley tradition was dead, America was de facto aligned with Britain, a money-centered power was in control of the nation's economy; a supporter of the Ku Klux Klan was in the White House—and America was preparing to enter World War I.

IV. Bertrand Russell's Monetarism

There is not a single university within the United States which today teaches economics, as economics as a physical science is defined by Gottfried Leibniz and Alexander Hamilton. The University graduates and the recipients of doctorates from Ivy League and related institutions have all actually been trained in Bertrand Russell-derived monetarism, not in economics.

This analysis of current-day monetarism was already accomplished twenty-four years ago in the basic textbook *So, You Wish to Learn all about Economics*[7] by Lyndon LaRouche, particularly in Chapter Seven, "A Chapter Dispensing with Monetary Theory." Therein, LaRouche states: "What passes for 'economics' in textbooks and professional journals today is essentially nothing more than monetary theory." Without recapitulating that entire chapter here, suffice it to say that LaRouche traces the roots of current British monetary theory back to Thomas Hobbes, Francis Bacon, and John Locke, and successively to the two following generations of David Hume, Adam Smith, and Jeremy Bentham, and then Thomas Malthus, James Mill, John Stuart Mill, and David Ricardo. It was this latter Nineteenth Century grouping who, in turn, became the immediate predecessors to the imperial Bertrand Russell.

Real vs. Fictitious Mathematical Wealth
The modern roots of today's monetarist outlook and financial speculation can all be traced back to the practices of the Bank of Amsterdam and the Amsterdam Bourse in the Seventeenth Century. After the Dutch invasion of Britain in 1688, those practices—in their entirety—were brought into London.

By the time of the Nineteenth Century emergence of British Liberalism, we already find a mature anti-human monetarist outlook, one in which people become mere commodities, and where "wealth" is defined by monetary profits, not an advancement in the human condition.

The revolution in human affairs at the beginning of the Twentieth Century ushered in the creation of some-

---

6. Between 1880 and the first World War, the United States was battered by a continuous series of London-created financial crises, including the Panics of 1884, 1893, and 1907. All of these Panics were brought about by severe credit contractions emanating from the Bank of England. During this time-frame British new capital issues accounted for 75% of all foreign investment in United States. Leading into the 1893 Panic, for example, new capital issues by the Bank of England went from £142.6 million in 1890 to 81.1 million in 1892, and 49.1 million in 1893. Investment collapsed, financial obligations could not be met, and businesses folded by the thousands. Between 1885 and 1888, there were 51,748 business failures, with liabilities of $757 million. In the 1907 Panic, another London-imposed policy of contraction and interest-rate hikes drained specie out of American markets. All of these crises were then used by Wall Street to justify their demands for monetary "reform," leading into the creation of the Federal Reserve.

So, You Wish to Learn All About Economics?

A Text on Elementary Mathematical Economics

by Lyndon H. LaRouche, Jr.

Lyndon LaRouche's university textbook on national economic policy, which also serves as a manual for government officials and advisors to governments.

Downloadable Kindle file $9.95

http://www.larouchepub.com

Product Code: BFBBK-1984-3-0-0-KINDLE

---

7. *So, You Wish to Learn all About Economics*, by Lyndon LaRouche, New Benjamin Franklin House, New York, 1984, available at *EIR*'s website.

thing even worse, a truly Satanic philosophy which destroyed not only economics, but poisoned virtually every aspect of our culture. Beginning with the work of David Hilbert and Bertrand Russell between 1900 and 1903, an attack was launched on the very nature of the human species itself. Hilbert and Russell argued that human creativity simply does not exist, and that all areas of science, economics, music, and every other field of human endeavor can be explained by dead mathematical formulas.[8]

It was the work of Hilbert and Russell which led directly into the Money System of the Twentieth Century, as well as virtually all of the modern schools of economics, which themselves are universally derived from the study of statistics, mathematical models, and probability theory. This approach pre-dates Russell, as, for example, with the publication in 1890 of the *Principles of Economics* by Alfred Marshall, whose work would have a profound influence on John Maynard Keynes. The so-called Austrian School also has its roots in the late Nineteenth Century, when it was actually created as a continental offshoot of the British School in order to do combat with the industrially-oriented Prussian School of Economics.

Nevertheless, after Bertrand Russell, the change was profound. Ludwig Von Mises published his *Theory of Money and Credit* in 1912, and John Maynard Keynes followed with his first book, *A Theory on Probability*, written in 1913 and published in 1921. This was a declaration of war against the human species. Economics was now defined as purely a mathematical construct of money. The Austrians and the Brits may have differed on approach and policy, but their axioms were (and still are) identical. Human creativity does not exist. Wealth is defined strictly in artificial monetary values. Probability theories and mathematical formulas will teach us how to maximize the extraction of profit from any system or market.

Completely absent is the Hamiltonian concept of human creativity and human progress. Completely absent is any consideration of the Human Mind. Completely absent is the reality of human invention, human discovery which has been the generator for all human advancement since the original mastery of the use of fire so many aeons ago.

8. See *Hilbert and Russell: The Suffocation of Science by Mathematics*, by Phil Rubinstein, *Executive Intelligence Review*, June 12, 2015, available here.

This mathematical fantasy, and the financial looting it is designed to perpetuate, is what the Federal Reserve System in the United States was created to serve. The tragedy is, that after 100 years of the Russellite influence, both these speculative financial institutions, as well as the "culture of money" within which they operate, are now universally pervasive in the trans-Atlantic world. People simply no longer know how to think about actual human wealth. They are simply stupid. Far more stupid than their great-great-grandparents.

V. Today—a New Harmony

Fortunately, an opportunity now exists to throw off this 100-plus year Dark Age. But it will not be easy.

On the positive side is the return not only to physical economics, but Hamiltonian science-driver economics, which has taken root in the development policies of the BRICS nations and the Shanghai Cooperation Organization. Nothing like this orientation has been seen in the world since the death of Franklin Roosevelt in 1945. Perhaps most exhilarating is the China-led *Return to the Moon*, a commitment to the human development of our Solar System, an expanding effort which now involves many nations—even some from among the poorest—from throughout the world. This is the path along which we as a species must proceed, *and these initiatives are happening*, now.

These efforts are the new *Harmony*, the modern reflection of the Lincoln-Grant-McKinley *Reciprocity* among nations, and it is within our reach to achieve it.

On the negative side, obviously there is the mental illness of the war-mongering President Obama, together with the blood-thirsty ambitions of the British Monarchy, which represent the most deadly threat to this new global orientation. But there is also the cultural obstacle. This has two aspects:

On the one hand, almost the entire population of Europe and North America, at least those under 80 years of age, have lived within a monetarist system their entire lives. They don't know anything else, and the younger they are, the worse the mental disease is. Lyndon LaRouche has pointed to the destruction of the Clinton Presidency and the subsequent fifteen years of the Bush and Obama Administrations, as a point of absolute downturn in the mental abilities of the American population. In American culture today there is no future orientation, no recognition of that creative human spark which sets us apart from the beasts, and no understanding whatsoever of economics. This is what 100 years of Bertrand Russell have brought us to.

At the same time, there is a tendency even among more intelligent, more courageous leaders to view actions such as the re-enactment of Glass-Steagall as "financial reforms." There is a reluctance, perhaps even among some of the BRICS leaders, to challenge the axioms of the Money System itself. What actually needs to be said is *"We will not be slaves to imaginary mathematical formulas; we are human beings, and we will take the necessary physical and scientific steps to secure future human development."* It remains to be seen if people will act in that direction.

PiB India

Indian Prime Minister Narendra Modi reflected the anti-monetarist spirit of the BRICS, when he told the crowd gathered at Madison Square Garden on Sept. 28, 2014 that India's 1.25 billion people were its wealth.

All money and all banks are creations of governments, creations of human beings. These institutions must be made to act in the interests of the human species. Failing that, they should either abolished or transformed by government action into something actually useful. They have no independent right to existence.

That is the fight. That is the challenge. It is no more difficult a challenge than that faced by Washington, or Lincoln, or Grant, which means it is a fight which can be won. And our *hope* of winning—as Friedrich Schiller understood the idea of *hope*—is much better today than it was yesterday.

This article was prepared with the assistance of Maureen McMichael and Dean Andromidas

Every Day Counts In Today's Showdown To Save Civilization

That's why you need EIR's **Daily Alert Service**, a strategic overview compiled with the input of Lyndon LaRouche, and delivered to your email 5 days a week.

For example: On Sept. 30 EIR's Daily Alert featured Lyndon LaRouche's warning that the action must be taken immediately to remove President Obama in order to not only avoid further provocations toward World War III, but to avoid a disorderly collapse of Wall Street.

"If Wall Street collapses in a debt panic, that chaotic destructive force can lead to death and destruction in the United States and around the world," he said. FDR's Glass-Steagall is needed now.

Russian President Vladimir Putin's recent initiative in Syria has weakened Obama and created the necessary opening to do what's needed. But time is of the essence.

This is intelligence you need to act on, if we are going to survive as a nation and a species. Can you really afford to be without it?

THURSDAY, OCTOBER 1, 2015

EIR Daily Alert Service

EIR DAILY ALERT SERVICE P.O. BOX 17390, WASHINGTON, DC 20041-0390

- LaRouche: Wall Street Must Be Shut Down Before It Crashes
- Kerry Confirms Shift in U.S. Policy on Syria, Assad
- Putin Orders First Air Strikes Against Syrian Jihadists
- Russia's Upper House Approves Use of Armed Forces Abroad
- German Government Rejects Turkish Proposal for 'Safe Zones' in Syria
- Senator Warren: Glass-Steagall 'Is Exactly What We Should Do'
- German Saving Banks Threatened by Zero Rates Policy and EU Over-Regulation
- Senator Feinstein Thinks Russia's Move in Syria May Be Positive
- Dana Rohrabacher, Chair, House Subcommittee on Europe, Eurasia, and Emerging Threats, Holds Hearing on Terrorist Threat in Russia
- Rep. Dana Rohrabacher Attacks U.S. Support of Saudis, and Campaign To Overthrow Assad in House Foreign Affairs Committee
- BRICS Foreign Ministers Meet in New York
- NASA May Join Chinese/European Space Science Mission
- Finding Water on Mars Provokes Broad Debate in China
- Secretary John Kerry Reviews the 2013 Powerful Example of Cooperating with

---

'Man-made Global Warming' Fraud Exposed at UN

On Sept. 22, the eve of the United Nations Summit on Sustainable Development, Executive Intelligence Review convoked a press conference/seminar at the United Nations to present its new special report " 'Global Warming' Scare Is Population Reduction, Not Science." We present here the two core presentations of that seminar, given by Benjamin Deniston of the LaRouche PAC Science team, and Thomas Wysmuller, of "The Right Climate Stuff," a NASA scientist and meteorologist. LaRouche PAC's Dennis Speed moderated the proceedings, which can be seen here in full.

Benjamin Deniston: My name is Benjamin Deniston. I wrote some sections of this report. I'm just going to give an overview of a few elements of the report. A lot of the details you can find in the report itself, but I want to just give a flavor of what we're discussing here today with this claim of a man-made climate catastrophe coming.

I think it's important just to start by clarifying the terms that are used, and the reality of the issue from some media publications right before this event. If you read the literal statements of these headlines (**Figure 1**), it's saying a certain specific thing. It's saying, "Obama Condemns Climate Change Deniers." "Bad News For Climate Change Deniers." "Climate Denier Group Likens Pope Climate Change Talk To Paganism."

Now this is a rather terrible misrepresentation of some of the scientific criticism that's being put forward, because many of the people opposing what's being pushed right now as a response to a supposed climate catastrophe, are not basing their arguments on denying the existence of climate change. And their arguments are not based on the idea of denying the existence of the climate itself, which some of these headlines seem to imply, by the way they phrase the wording here. What is being addressed here is something rather different.

It's one thing to recognize climate change exists. We recognize that climate changes. We recognize human beings have been emitting large amounts of carbon dioxide. We recognize carbon dioxide is a greenhouse gas that can have an effect on the climate. Those are pretty well-established facts.

It is another issue to claim that the human release of greenhouse gases is the predominant cause of the increase in temperature of the past century. It is another statement to say the continued release of CO_2 will cause catastrophic effects for the planet, and then

FIGURE 1

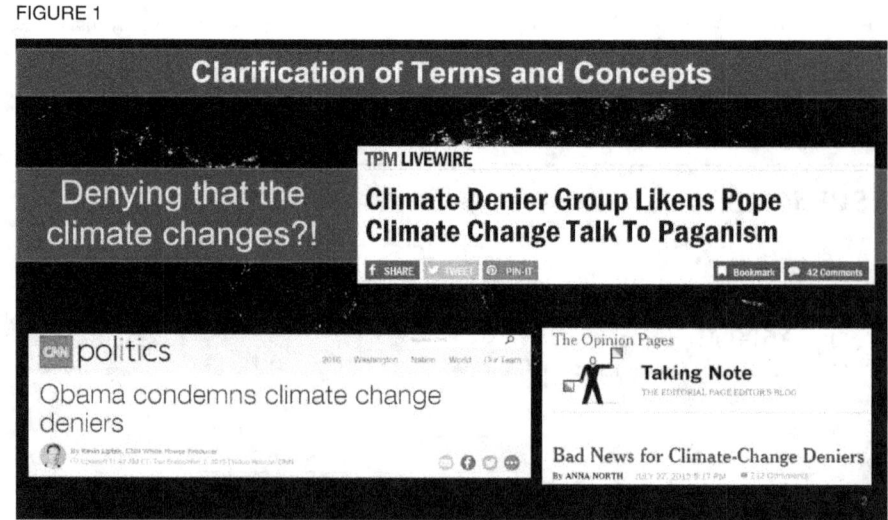

FIGURE 2

Clarification of Terms and Concepts

A big difference:

- Human release of greenhouse gasses is the predominate cause of increasing temperature for the recent half century

- Continued human release of CO2 will cause catastrophic effects (warming, worse storms, sea level rise, etc.)

- It will be best for human society to take drastic action to dramatically reduce CO2 emissions

FIGURE 3

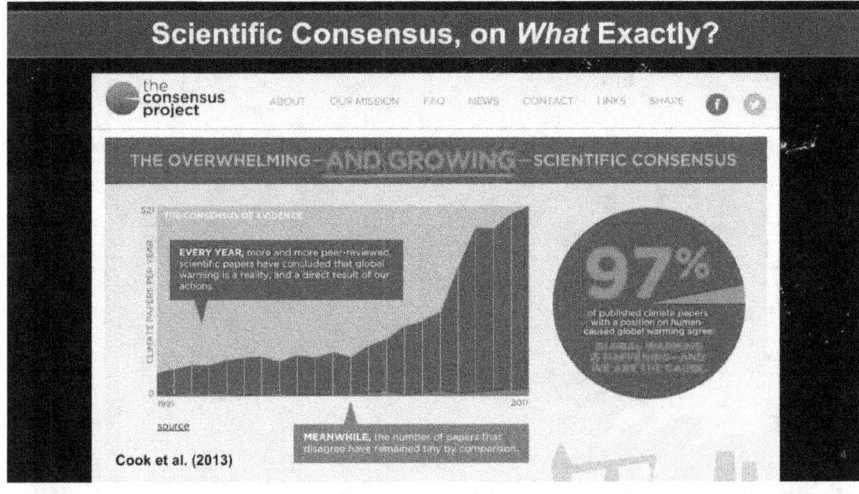

Scientific Consensus, on *What* Exactly?

Cook et al. (2013)

FIGURE 4

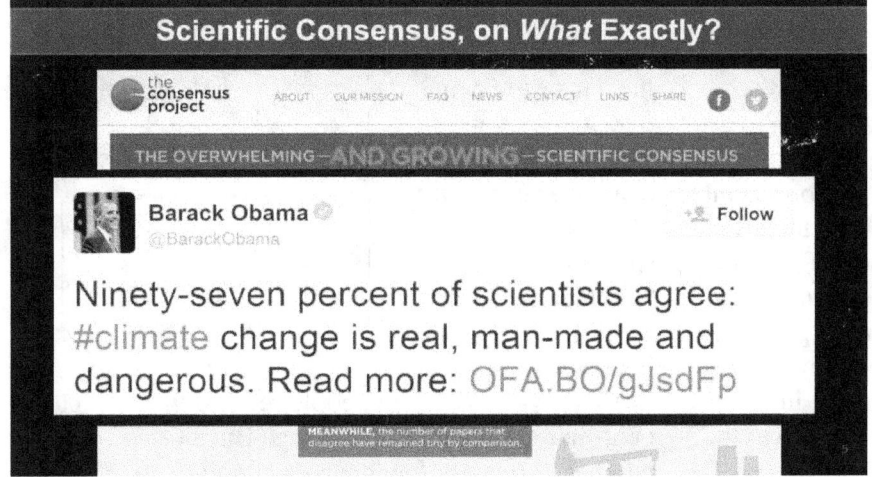

Scientific Consensus, on *What* Exactly?

Barack Obama · @BarackObama · Follow

Ninety-seven percent of scientists agree: #climate change is real, man-made and dangerous. Read more: OFA.BO/gJsdFp

there's another thing to say, it will be best for human society to take drastic action to dramatically reduce CO_2 emissions.

This is what we're taking issue with. We're not saying, CO_2 isn't potentially a small effect on the climate. **What we're taking issue with is the claim that human CO_2 emissions are having catastrophic effects that require dramatic action, to have major interventions to change our mode of existence to deal with.** That's what's being addressed here. (**Figure 2**)

The Phony Consensus

Now, just to put this up front, there is often talk of a "consensus" in the scientific community over the issue of climate change. And this is a website called The Consensus Project. (**Figure 3**) It's based on a 2013 study, which claimed to show that there's a 97% consensus in the scientific community, in the climate community, over the issue of climate change.

Again, we have this distinction I just made, comes back up here, because this is often presented, as evidence presented by the President of the United States, for example. Barack Obama presented evidence saying that the majority of scientists agree, not just with the existence of climate change, not just with the existence of humans having an effect, but the claim that humans are causing catastrophic effects, that need to be dealt with immediately. (**Figure 4**)

Now other scientists have actually looked at the studies that were cited in this report, this report that claimed the 97% consensus. Other people have gone back and reviewed what works were supposedly going into that consensus. I've cited here the peer-reviewed published paper on the subject here in the slide. You can also go to this website called which has posted a nice list of 97 articles refuting this supposed consensus.

What was found when people looked back at this paper, was that after they reviewed almost 12,000 climate papers, only 41 of those 12,000 climate papers explicitly agreed with the statement that man is causing most of the warming since 1950. (**Figure 5**) So the consensus was that 97% agreed that humans are emitting CO_2, and that CO_2 has some effect on the climate! That's not a controversial claim. That was what most of these papers agreed to.

What was not a consensus by any means in these academic studies, was the claim that humans are *causing* most of the warming. Far less than 1% of the papers explicitly made a statement on that; and said that we're having such an effect that we need to take dramatic actions to reduce CO_2 emissions in the very short term. There are more details in the report, but I just want to put this out here to alleviate some of the misinformation that's been presented, as if there's a complete consensus on the issue of this being an emergency that we have to deal with immediately. That is not the case.

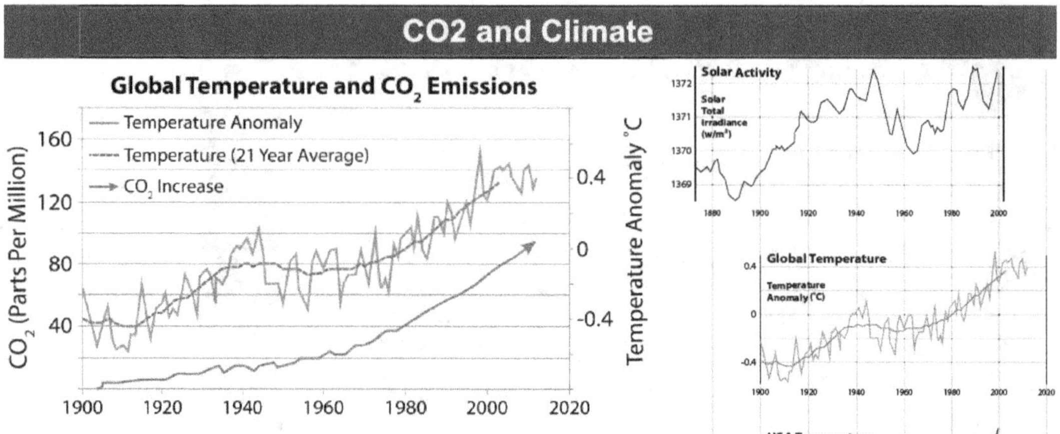

Carbon Dioxide and Climate

With this stated, I want to take a few minutes to go over the issue of the relation between carbon dioxide and temperature. Again this is presented in more detail in the report. But we're often presented with the argument that carbon dioxide is a major driver of climate, that the climate is incredibly responsive or sensitive to changes in CO_2 levels. It is the case over the past century, that we've seen general increasing amount of CO_2 in the atmosphere; and we've seen a general increase in temperature since around the 1950s, 1960s, up to the turn of the century. (**Figure 6**)

FIGURE 5

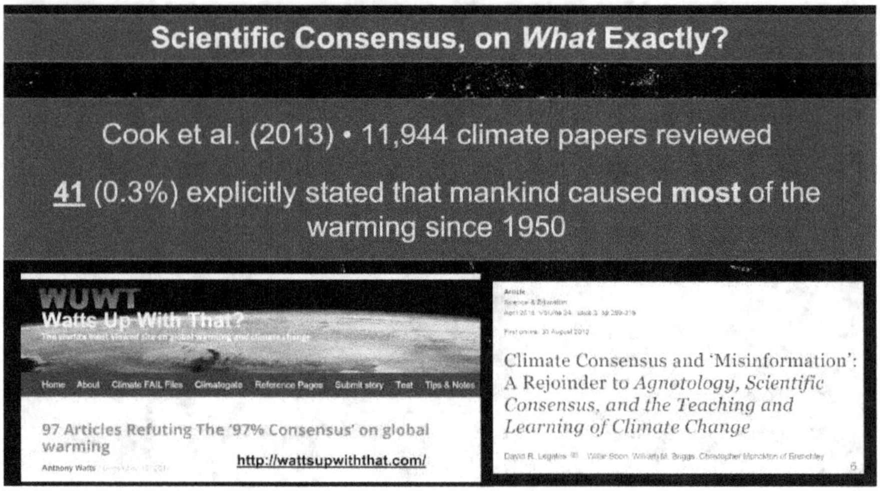

Scientific Consensus, on *What* Exactly?

Cook et al. (2013) • 11,944 climate papers reviewed

41 (0.3%) explicitly stated that mankind caused **most** of the warming since 1950

WUWT
Watts Up With That?

97 Articles Refuting The '97% Consensus' on global warming

http://wattsupwiththat.com/

Climate Consensus and 'Misinformation': A Rejoinder to *Agnotology, Scientific Consensus, and the Teaching and Learning of Climate Change*

FIGURE 6

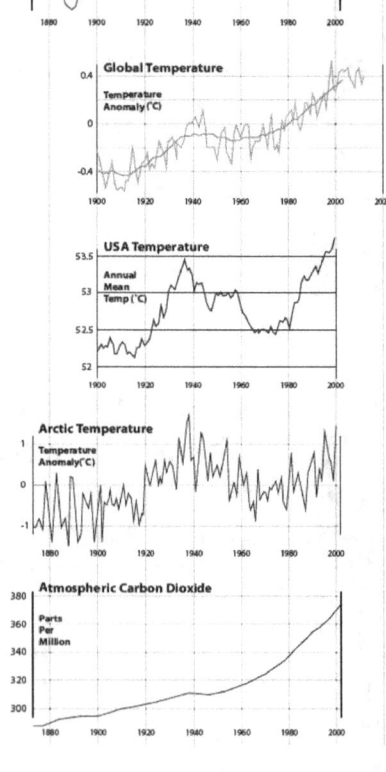

CO2 and Climate

Global Temperature and CO₂ Emissions
— Temperature Anomaly
--- Temperature (21 Year Average)
→ CO₂ Increase

Since the late '90s we've had a flat-line in global temperature. These are two different assessments of satellite measurements of global atmospheric temperature over the past 18-plus years, and they show that the global temperature on average has not been increasing; it's flatlined. (**Figure 7**) Some people refer to this as a pause, or a hiatus, in global warming. But this is one of a number of pieces of evidence that point very clearly to

FIGURE 7

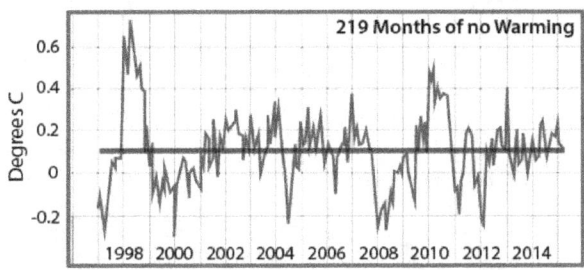

FIGURE 8

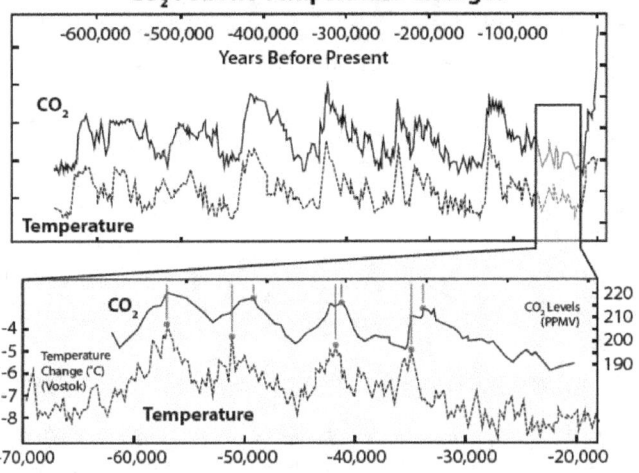

Measurements of temperature and CO_2 for the past 600,000 years. Image adapted from "Analysis of ice core data from Antarctica," by Indermühle et al. (GRL, vol. 27, p. 735, 2000), and the science fiction film An Inconvenient Truth.

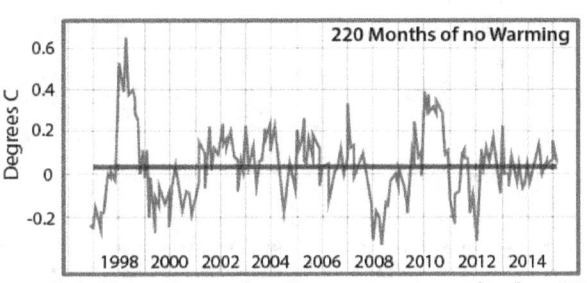

Satellite measurements show that global temperature remains flat while CO_2 emissions have continued to accelerate.

FIGURE 9

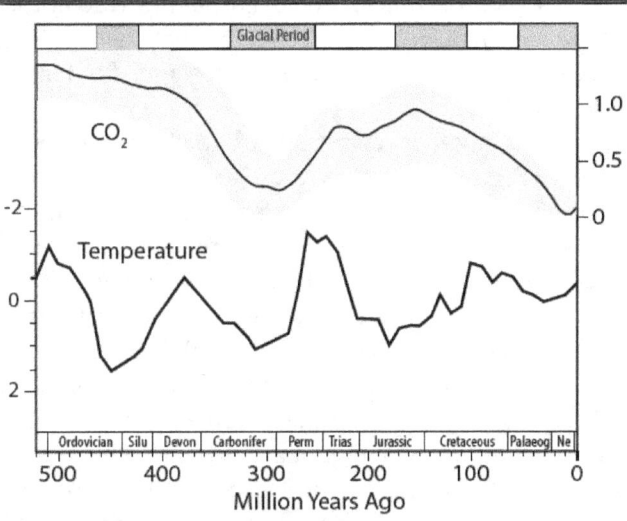

Temperature and CO_2 levels for the past 500 million years. Image adapted from Berner and Kothavala, 2001 and Veizer et al., 2001.

the reality that the atmospheric system, the climate system, the global temperature, are not highly sensitive, or highly responsive to CO_2 emissions. Over the past 20 years we've been putting more CO_2 into the atmosphere than we ever have before, and we're not seeing a warming trend in the atmosphere as a response.

I want to show this as another presentation of this issue, because Al Gore had used this graphic in his science-fiction video, "An Inconvenient Truth," which showed a correlation between CO_2 and temperature for the past half-million years, the past 600,000 years. He claimed it as evidence that the temperature is highly sensitive to CO_2, that CO_2 itself is a major driver of what the global climate, the global temperature does. And as you can see in the top graphic, yes, it's clear that there's a correlation between CO_2 and temperature. **(Figure 8)**

However, what Al Gore did not say, and what many of the alarmists have not said and will not admit, unless pressed on the issue, is that a number of studies have shown very clearly that the CO_2 changes for this entire period come *after* the changes in temperature. So this is not at all evidence that changes in CO_2 levels drive temperature changes or climate changes, but quite the opposite. It's showing us that the CO_2 levels in the atmosphere tend to respond to a change in climate, which is being changed by other factors.

If you go back further—this graphic **(Figure 9)** is

FIGURE 10

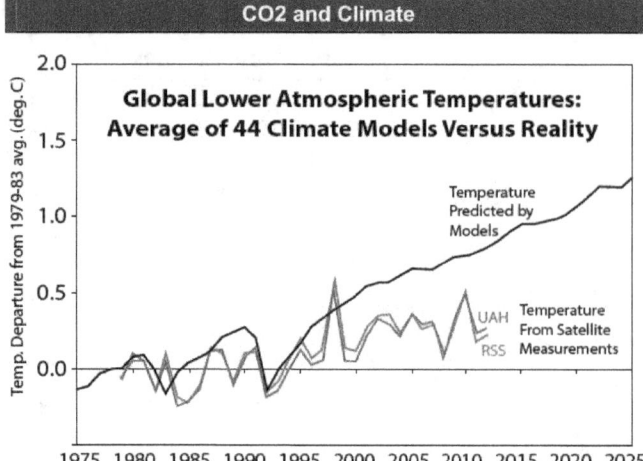

"The global temperature predicted by an average of 44 climate models compared against actual global temperatures measured by satellites. Image adapted from Dr. Roy Spencer, "95% of Climate Models Agree: The Observations Must be Wrong," February 7th, 2014, http://www.drroyspencer.com/

FIGURE 11

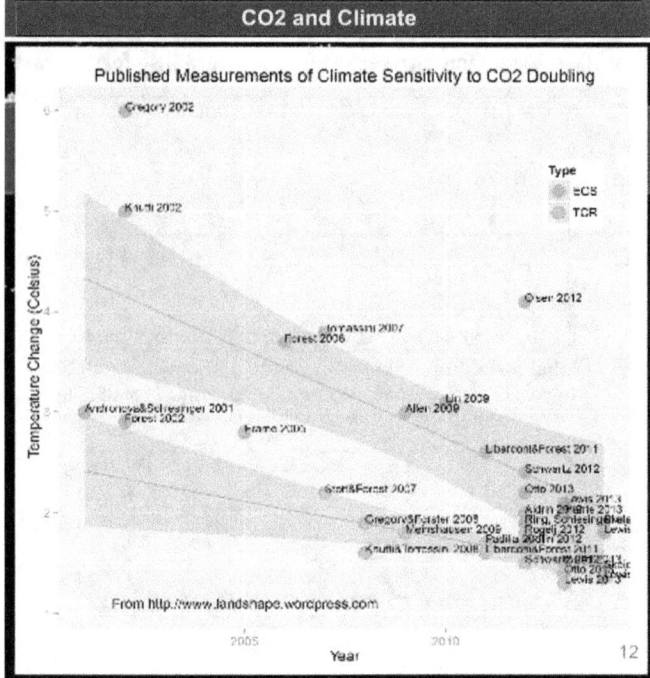

David Stockwell https://landshape.wordpress.com/2015/06/20/6921/

going back a very long time period, the past half-billion years, the past 500 million years, in an attempt to get some type of estimate of temperature changes and CO_2 changes over this time period. And again, we do not see a clear causal correlation. We see periods when CO_2 is increasing and temperature is decreasing, for tens of millions of years.

Here is another, coming back to the more recent period. (**Figure 10**) Again, these are lines of evidence showing us that we don't have any clear proof that the atmosphere is as sensitive or as responsive to CO_2 levels as we're supposedly being led to believe. This is a comparison that's been made with the predictions by climate models for what they would forecast global temperature to be doing, under the influence of rising CO_2 levels compared with measurements from satellite instrumentation of the global average temperature. Again, we're seeing a very large deviation now, between what the actual temperature is doing and what is being claimed it should do, under the false assumption, the false belief, that the atmospheric system is highly sensitive, or highly responsive, to CO_2 levels.

Here's another interesting graphic. (**Figure 11**) This is a plot of various academic papers, which have been published on the subject of how sensitive is the atmosphere to changes in CO_2 levels. On the bottom axis, this time we're going from around 2000 to 2015, and the vertical axis shows us basically how much we

would believe the temperature should change, if the CO_2 levels doubled. As we can see, even in the "climate community," even in the climate literature, we're seeing a dramatic reduction in the assessment of how sensitive the climate is to CO_2 levels.

I want to just present this, because all this comes together in painting a very clear picture that, again, we recognize CO_2 levels are increasing. We recognize CO_2 is a greenhouse gas that can have some effect on the atmosphere. But then to make the leap to say that what we know to be the coming human emissions of CO_2 will cause some catastrophic activity—sea-level rise, increased storms, major temperature increase, droughts, all these things you see on the news headlines—the connection between human CO_2 emissions and these extreme, catastrophic statements, is not there. It's not in the scientific consensus; it's not in what's been scientifically demonstrated. It may exist in some climate models, where it exists because it was put in as an assumption from the start.

The actual evidence is not showing us that the climate is so incredibly sensitive to CO_2 emissions, that we should be taking dramatic actions in lowering CO_2 emissions, stopping using coal, stopping using gasoline, activities which will have, as Dennis discussed in the opening, serious catastrophic consequences on the livelihood, the well-being, the economic viability of populations and nations around the world.

That's what I wanted to just present, to open up here. And do you want to introduce Tom? And then we're going to have our next speaker.

Speed: Our next speaker is Tom Wysmuller. He's a trained meteorologist at NYU, worked at NASA for five years. He works with a group of former NASA employees, astronauts and others. They call themselves the Right Climate Stuff Club. So, Tom.

Some Straight Talk On Sea-Level Rise

Tom Wysmuller: All right, well, actually we're a group mainly centered at the Johnson Space Center…[technical interruption]

What you're going to be seeing here are some slides that are a sub-set of a much larger presentation that I'll be giving at the 10th Annual Water Conference that's going to be held in Bulgaria in a couple of weeks. I think if you google "water conference bulgaria" http://www.waterconf.org/, you'll find it.[1]

Anyway, what you are seeing here is what many people are saying is going to be the future for New York City. (**Figure 12**) Turns out that this is a cover of a book by Heidi Cullen, and the fact is, this isn't going to happen in anybody's lifetime, at all. It's a scare. It makes people get anxious about climate change and CO_2. It is not the future for New York City.

What you're seeing on this graphic (**Figure 13**) is the great ice sheet that covered North America, sometimes one and two miles thick during the last 100,000 years, but it started melting around 18,000 years ago. Right here you see a lake. This is not the Great Salt Lake in Utah. This is Lake Bonneville. Lake Bonneville was held in place by an ice dam, or an alluvial fan, but it broke open, and for about a year, it literally flooded the oceans with the water that was coming out of that ice sheet as it melted.

You're looking here at the sea-level history. (**Figure 14**) And you notice right here about 18,000 years ago,

---

1. Mr. Wysmuller's presentation at the Bulgarian Water Conference is entitled "Sea-Level Rise, Tide Gauges/Satellites—Different Linear Measures, Inconsistent Results, & Apparently Unaffected by Recent CO2 Increases."

FIGURE 12

Sea-Level Rise
Is this the future for NYC?

FIGURE 13

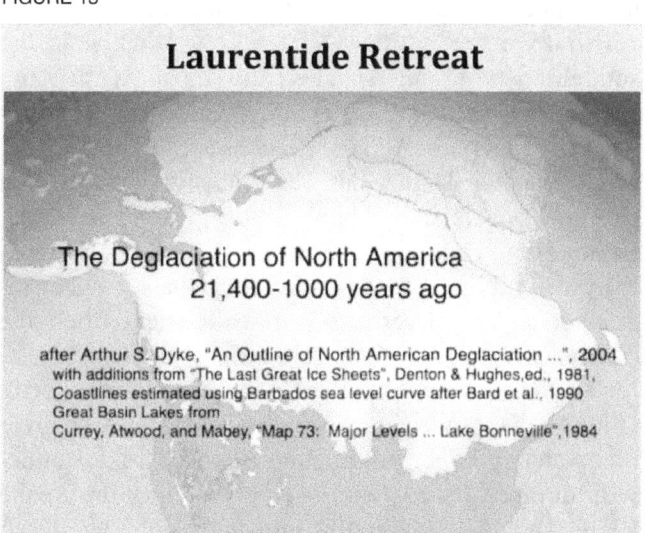

Laurentide Retreat

The Deglaciation of North America
21,400-1000 years ago

after Arthur S. Dyke, "An Outline of North American Deglaciation …", 2004 with additions from "The Last Great Ice Sheets", Denton & Hughes,ed., 1981, Coastlines estimated using Barbados sea level curve after Bard et al., 1990 Great Basin Lakes from Currey, Atwood, and Mabey, "Map 73: Major Levels … Lake Bonneville",1984

sea levels started rising, as that ice sheet melted. So during this period, from the last inter-glacial, down to 18,000 years ago that ice sheet was building up, accumulating more and more snow and ice. Long Island, which is right around here, is the terminal moraine, or end point of that last glacier. What happened is that when the glacier was formed, it moved south. It didn't move like a snowplow. It didn't push things in front of it. What it did, it may have encapsulated a rock in northern Quebec, and then as the ice sheet moved south, that rock was transported, and at the southern end, it termi-

FIGURE 14

Sea-Level History

FIGURE 15

7,500 Year Spike

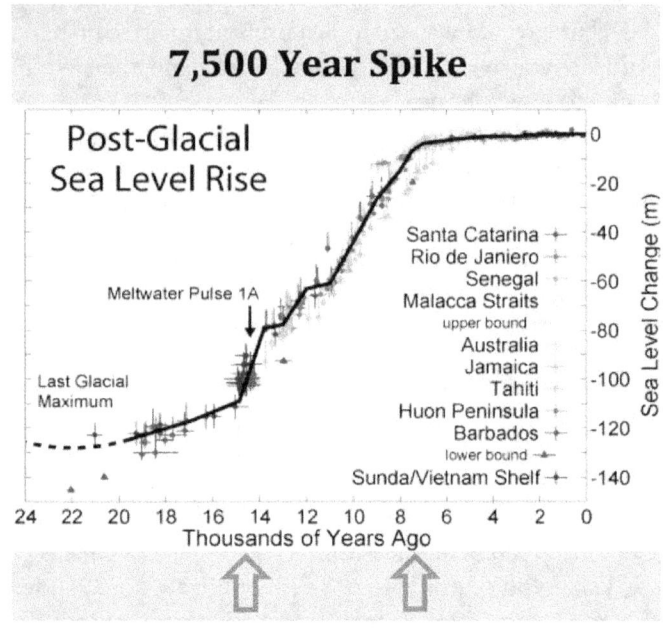

FIGURE 16

IPCC SLR "Pathways"

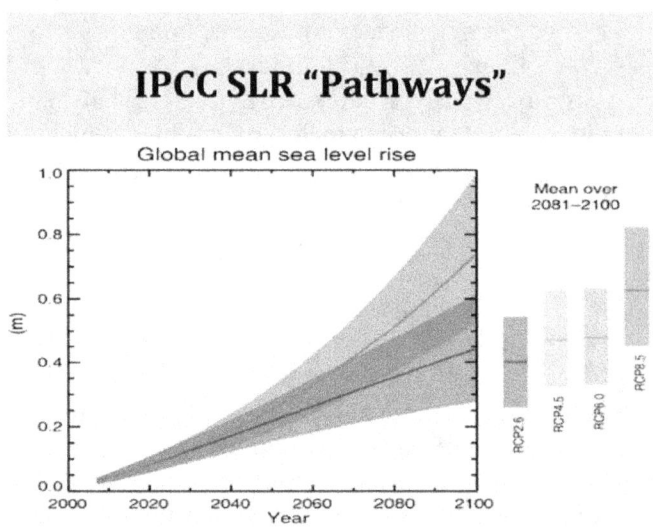

nated, and the ice melts, and leaves the rock.

So if you are familiar with the Long Island area, the southern part of Long Island is called an out-wash plain. It is flat as a pancake. It's great to build airports; that's where JFK is built. And the beaches tend to be the sand that's left over from what was dragged. The northern part of Long Island is lumpy. You go by places like Huntington, you have 200-foot hills, which are basically the rubble that was left. Then the ice sheet retreated, and as it retreated, it melted and filled the oceans, and that's what you are seeing here.

The next slide will have a little bit more detail. (**Figure 15**) Between the arrows is what I call the great meltwater spike, or pulse. Here is where Lake Bonneville dumped its contents over a year into the Snake River, and then eventually into the Columbia River. And you see a sharp upwards spike. So here the ice starts melting. Spike here, a couple of other spikes. And then finally, about 8,000 years ago, the sea level rise kind of flattens out. Now, why does it flatten out? Maybe because all the ice is gone! The great ice sheet has already melted. So sea level is flat. And it is flat basically until this day.

Now you notice there is still a slight upward rise, and here is the key. Global warming, in the sense of oceans getting warmer, is real. The oceans are accumulating heat, and the thermal expansion, without more ice coming into the ocean, allows the ocean to slightly

rise. And you'll see that fairly clearly in a few more slides.

The Scare-Mongers

Now, unfortunately, here are the scare tactics. (**Figure 16**) The IPCC has sea-level rise pathways; they're called representative concentration pathways, and they're all dependent on the amount of CO_2 that gets put into the air. So within this century, they're expecting a one meter sea-level rise with current or ex-

FIGURE 17

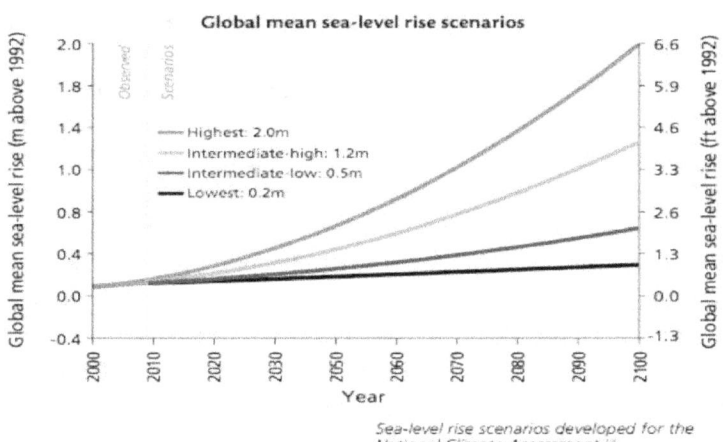

FIGURE 18

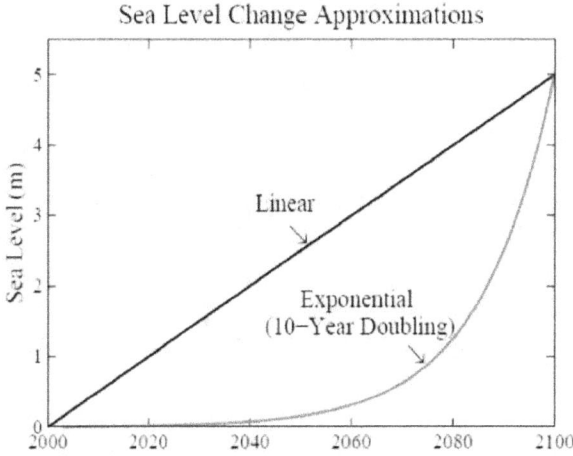

Five-meter sea level change in 21ˢᵗ century under assumption of linear change and exponential change (Hansen, 2007), the latter with a 10-year doubling time.

pected emissions of CO_2. The other targets are reductions, but you notice they're all rising.

Well, our Administration decided to go one better. The National Climate Assessment (**Figure 17**) said, "Nah, the IPCC is wrong. We're going to go 2 meters up!" Basically 6.6 feet. Again, here's where we are, flat, and even this line here is *double* the increase of the last century, that we've experienced. And again, the pathways are different, depending on the CO_2 emissions.

Now we're going to see there's not a lot of linkage there. When, it turns out, Jim Hansen was talking to a reporter in 1988, standing in his office; and the reporter says, "What are you expect to see in the next 50 years, or so?" And Jim Hansen looks out the window and says, "You're going to see a lot more traffic." And the reporter said, "Well, how come?" He said, "Well, you see the West Side Highway [in Manhattan], which is on the other side of that road, is going to be flooded. You're going to have sea-level rise to such an extent, that all of the traffic is going to be spilled over, into the city streets. And there will be other things going wrong too." I won't go over the whole article.

Well, it turned out—and by the way, this was predicated on a doubling of the pre-industrial CO_2 levels. Well, CO_2 levels are about half-way there now, from when Jim Hansen was talking, about maybe 40%. The actual sea-level rise along the West Side Highway is not 10 feet, which would have inundated it, like he said. It's

1 inch. So, 1 inch. We have 25 more years for his prediction to come true, to get the other 9 feet, 11 inches. It's not going to happen, folks.

Originally they had a linear relationship of the sea-level rise. Well, Jim Hansen got real smart; he's a good mathematician, and he figured, "Uh-oh, this is not working," so he created this exponential curve in 2007, (**Figure 18**) which basically tracks exactly what's happening now! We have really no sea-level rise, and then he expects in the last 20 years for it to sky-rocket for another 15 feet, or 16 feet. That's not going to happen either, folks.

The Reality

Here are some local effects in New York City. (**Figure 19**) The press comes to New York; you notice in New York City, in the Battery, you have a steady rise in sea-level. And the same with Boston, particularly after 1961, which is right here. Boston kind of shoots up. Now, what's happened in Boston? They have 19 new skyscrapers, built in Boston, since 1960, over what's called frangible bedrock. So basically, Boston is being pressed down by the buildings; Boston is sinking, and they're saying, "Gee, look at that. We have accelerating sea-level in Boston."

New York is a little bit different. New York has a *very* steady rise, but it is about double the world sea-

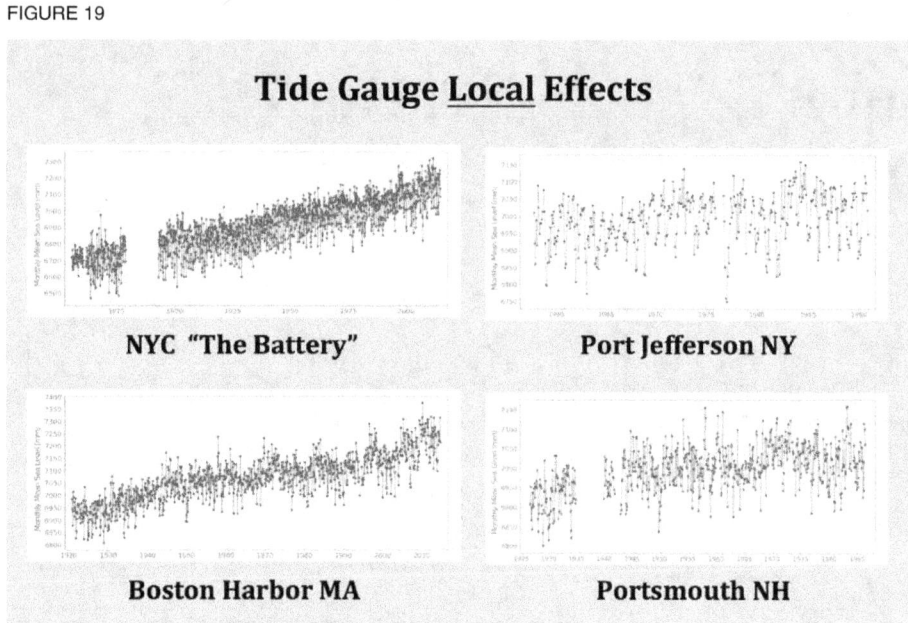

FIGURE 19

Tide Gauge <u>Local</u> Effects

NYC "The Battery"

Port Jefferson NY

Boston Harbor MA

Portsmouth NH

level rise. Why? Look outside the window here. You got all these skyscrapers, all these buildings. They're on bedrock, but that bedrock rests on something called the asthenosphere, which is a layer between magma, that will create volcanoes—we don't have any of those here—but it basically allows this bedrock, which we are putting these huge buildings on, to press down, slowly but surely. So we experience sea-level rise.

I've got Port Jeff [Port Jefferson, Long Island] here: Port Jeff is in the same ocean, and this is a subset of this particular graphic, and Port Jeff really is not showing

very much sea-level rise at all. And the same thing with Boston and Portsmouth, New Hampshire. Portsmouth is about 60 miles north of Boston. Sea level is fairly flat in the same period, that Boston is accelerating, because Portsmouth doesn't have any skyscrapers.

If you go to Portland, Maine, the tide gauge in Portland, Maine today registers *exactly* what it registered in 1947. *No* sea-level rise. Now, in truth, there's been a slight rise. In 1947, we're taking one of the higher points, not the highest point; and the current happened to be fairly low, but the old-timers in Maine just say, "The sea-level's not going up," and they're right! And Portland, Maine, is an area which is tectonically inert, meaning it is neither rising nor falling.

I'm going to be showing you a slide about a tectonically inert place. This is actually the good way to look at it. (**Figure 20**) This is by Axel Mörner, a brilliant oceanographer from Scandinavia. And what Mörner does, he takes the areas which are getting uplifted, and he takes the areas that are experiencing subsidence; obviously in the areas that are sinking, they are noting a sea-level rise, and the places that are rising, there's not that many of them, but there are some in Alaska and the West Coast where the sea level is not rising; it's actually falling.

The actual statistic you want to look for is in the middle. It's the ones that are not rising, not falling, and the rise is quite gradual, and mainly due to thermal expansion of the oceans. There is some glacial meltwater coming in, but it is very minimal. Again, the great Laurentide Glacier has long gone. And by the way, I can give you citations to the paper that this shows up in, so you can get a really good clean graphic. OK? For the people in the press who keep on taking the pictures of it. [laughter]

Where's the Temperature Rise?

Here is a graphic taken from the National Climate Assessment, (**Figure 21**) and it shows

FIGURE 20

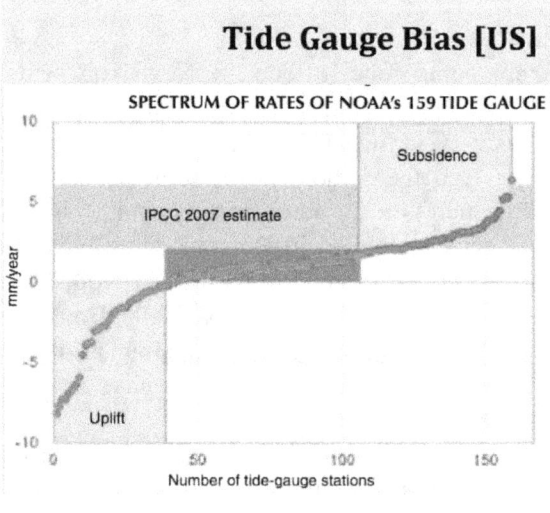

Tide Gauge Bias [US]

SPECTRUM OF RATES OF NOAA's 159 TIDE GAUGE STATIONS

The values of NOAA's 159 tide gauge stations indicate that they range from uplifted areas to subsiding areas (green areas). If the uplifting and subsiding sites (green areas) are excluded, we are left with a number of sites (red area) where the rise in sea level ranges between 0.0 and 2.0 mm/year. This is considerably below the rate given by IPCC (pink area) and satellite altimetry (as discussed below).

FIGURE 21

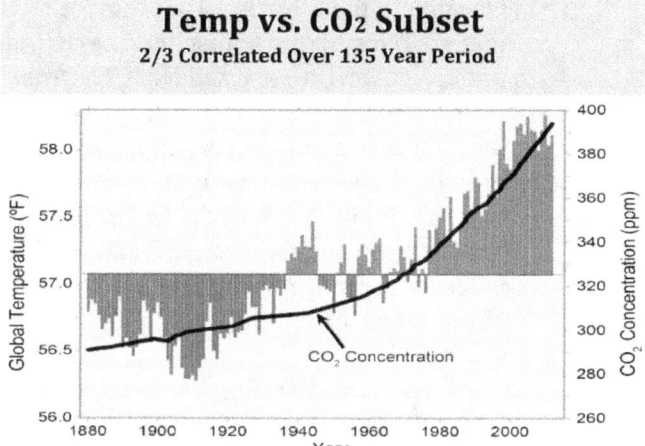

Temp vs. CO₂ Subset

2/3 Correlated Over 135 Year Period

FIGURE 22

2000 yr. Temp vs. CO₂

4.5% Correlation!!! – Black Arrow = Subset

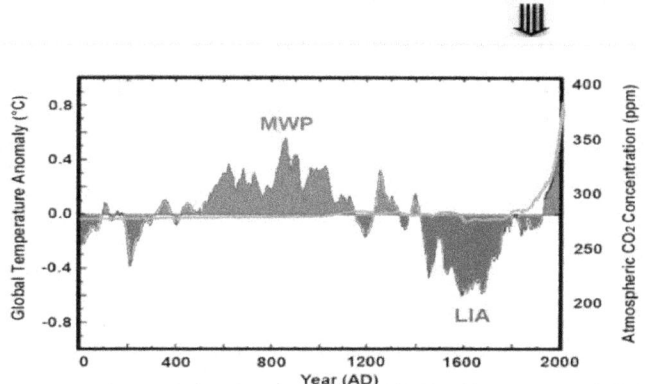

CO₂ going up from 1880, into the present. The graphic has a tiny little nitpick mistake in here, because we are actually in this flat-line area now. The British call it a stand-still, as far as temperature goes. But, be as it may, this is still pretty accurate.

Now, notice down here, temperature is going *down*, as CO₂ goes up. So this is only correlated for two-thirds of its entire term. Since the Industrial Revolution, we humans have put carbon dioxide into the atmosphere, and nobody is really going on a different path with that; I think we kind of agree on it. But the impact is not quite what you look at. You have some temperature drops here also; CO₂ is going up. Here you have decent correlation, but correlation is *not* causation, and that's the key.

So I call this a subset. Why? Because I'm going to go back now 2,000 years, and the green line is CO₂ for the last 2,000 years. (**Figure 22**) Under this little black arrow is the subset that you saw before. Right? So you can see, there is a similarity in that little subset. So here you have CO₂ tracking straight as an arrow: Medieval warm period, temperatures sky-rocket; the Little Ice Age, they plummet. *CO₂ and temperature are just not linked.*

Here, we get lucky, because we're putting CO₂ into the air, as temperatures are rising. We didn't have that happen here. Temperatures rose here, CO₂ didn't rise. The linkage between CO₂ is, in this case, less than 4.5%

FIGURE 23

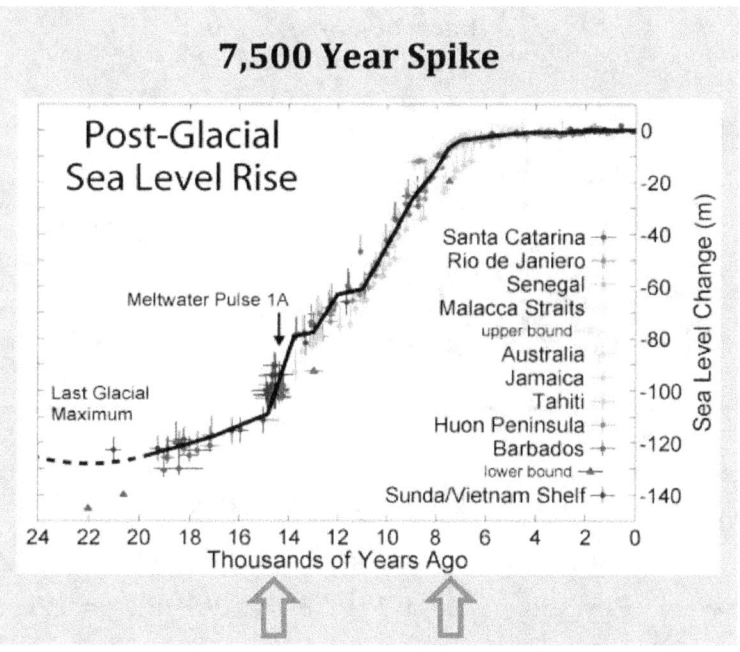

7,500 Year Spike

correlated. That is not one driving the other, by *any* stretch of anybody's imagination!

Here is your sea level now; that was temperature, you notice. (**Figure 23**) This is sea level: Again, sea level is relatively flat, just slightly rising because of thermal expansion, and some more glacial melt. This is CO₂. Now this is the Keeling Curve. (**Figure 24**) It varies. You see these little spiky things? They go up and down like a sawtooth. The Keeling Curve is

FIGURE 24

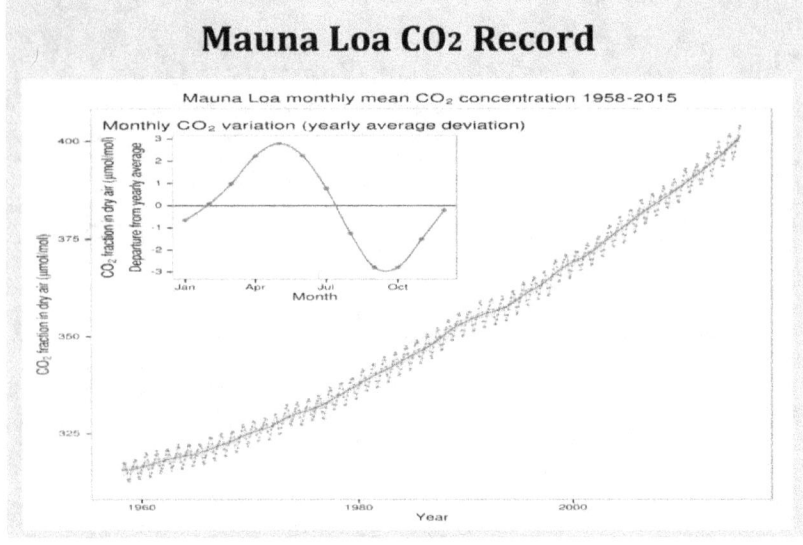

Mauna Loa CO₂ Record

Mauna Loa monthly mean CO₂ concentration 1958-2015

FIGURE 25

Effect of Agung
Volcano on World CO₂

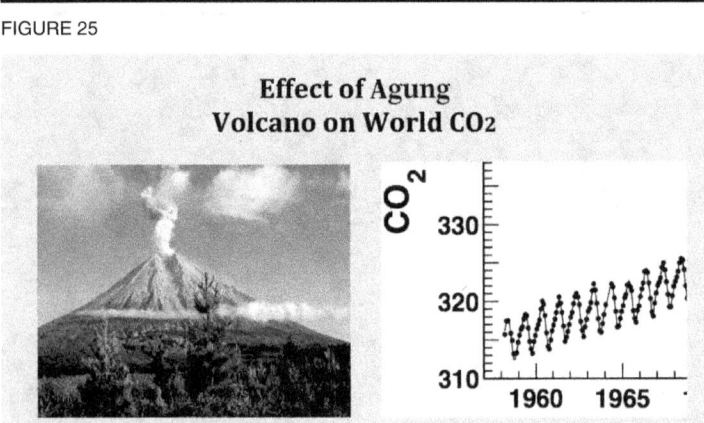

FIGURE 26

GHGs by Source & %

Source	N + H = T - ReA = I
Percent	97 + 3 = 100-98.5 = 1.5

Table 3. Global Natural and Anthropogenic Sources and Absorption of Greenhouse Gases in the 1990s

Gas	Sources			Absorption	Annual Increase in Gas in the Atmosphere
	Natural	Human-Made	Total		
Carbon Dioxide (Million Metric Tons of Gas)[a]	770,000	23,100	793,100	781,400	11,700
Methane (Million Metric Tons of Gas)[b]	239	359	598	576	22
Nitrous Oxide (Million Metric Tons of Gas)[c]	9.5	6.9	16.4	12.6	3.8

Emissions of Greenhouse Gases in the United States 2004

Energy Information Administration
Office of Integrated Analysis and Forecasting
U.S. Department of Energy

Source: Intergovernmental Panel on Climate Change, Climate Change 2001: The Scientific Basis (Cambridge, UK: Cambridge University Press, 2001).

http://tonto.eia.doe.gov/FTPROOT/environment/057304.pdf

mainly Northern Hemisphere-oriented. It's on Hawaii. It's in the Scripps Howard Institute. It's in the middle of the Pacific Ocean, but the effects of CO_2 they're feeling are Northern Hemisphere. And you notice, in April, all of a sudden, CO_2 *drops!* It drops like a rock. And it drops because the plants are sucking in CO_2. They are growing. The trees are getting leaves on them again. In October, the leaves fall. It's harvest time and then sea level rises. How is sea level rising? Mainly through oceanic out-gassing; I'm going to get into that in a second.

But a couple of things I want to point out in the Keeling Curve. Number one, there are some places where CO_2 actually drops. Right here, a three-year drop. This happens to coincide with the giant volcano Agung in Indonesia, which erupted, and basically blanketed the upper stratosphere with ash, dust, preventing sunlight from coming in, hitting the ocean, serving as nuclei for water vapor to form and create clouds, which again would reflect energy coming in. So the oceans didn't warm that much, and CO_2 flat-lined, or actually dropped. So again, oceanic out-gassing is that factor.

Up here again, Pinatubo in the Philippines did the same thing; it didn't quite drop CO_2, but came pretty close. And by the way, once the volcanic ash settles out of the atmosphere, everything's back to normal, CO_2 continues rising.

Here is Agung. That's a picture of it, (**Figure 25**) and here you can see the drop. Now I'm going to use this little subset, because I'm going to be talking about the increase from year to year in CO_2. You notice here again, this is April, then you have September, October, and then you have a slightly higher area (See Figure 24). And again, that is the increase, the annual increase in CO_2. And it turns out to be about 1.5%. Now let's see how that works.

No Evidence of Causation

This is a fairly complicated graphic, and I want to walk through it slowly, so you understand what's going on here.

FIGURE 27

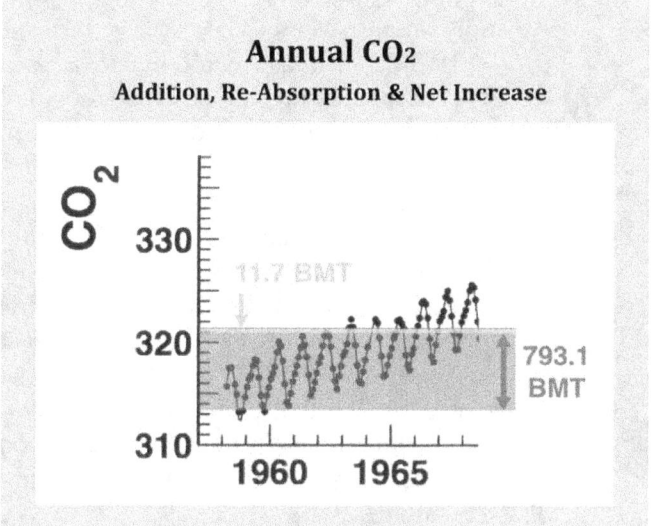

Annual CO₂

Addition, Re-Absorption & Net Increase

FIGURE 28

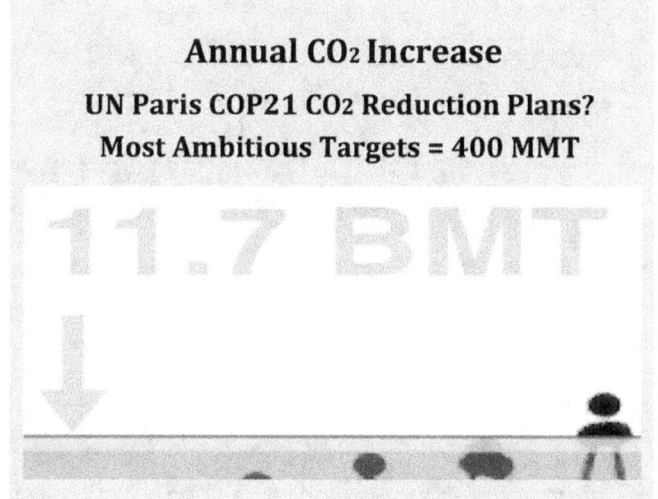

Annual CO₂ Increase

UN Paris COP21 CO₂ Reduction Plans?

Most Ambitious Targets = 400 MMT

This is from the IPCC report, and it goes over the sources for greenhouse gasses (**Figure 26**). And I'm going to concentrate on carbon dioxide, because that is the largest contributor, even though methane is about 20 to 23 times as much heat trapping, its effect is quite minimal. And you have natural sources, and again, this is mainly out-gassing from the oceans. As the oceans warm, they kick out the heavier CO_2 molecules that are dissolved in them, and they enter the atmosphere.

Humans do pretty well here. They get 23 million metric tons of CO_2. The total is 793 million, and the absorption at the end of the year, is 781. So what's left? The annual increase is 11.7—that's it. And most of it is probably due to humans. Now, I'm saying most, not all; because as the oceans warm, they are going to be kicking out more CO_2. And since the oceans, except for the Southern Ocean, are all still warming, you have that effect.

I'm going to go back, looking again on top, natural, 97% of all emissions of CO_2 come from nature. And by the way, plants exhale CO_2 at night. In humans, 3%; the total is 100%, and re-absorption is 98.5%. And this graphic here shows 1.5% is what's left over. The average over the years of the Keeling Curve, is about 1.49%, since they started taking it in Hawaii.

Now let's see what the effect is. I've tried to do it graphically here. (**Figure 27**) So here you see, the bottom here, and you have CO_2 going up in the Fall.

April comes, and then the net increase is this thin blue line you see right here. So you have 11 billion metric tons increase in a year; 793 [million] is the difference. And again I can go back here. Here is your 11 billion, and your 793, which is the total.

Let's try this one now. The biggest reduction plans that we can *possibly* hope for, as a result of the Paris talks (**Figure 28**), are a 400 million metric ton reduction in CO_2. That's significant; I'm not going to deny it. However, the 11 billion is the increase that you saw from the last graphic; the 400 million metric doesn't even fit within this thin line. It is *that* minuscule.

The point I'm trying to make is that the reduction plans that we're hoping for CO_2 are *almost* not measurable.

And here is the key graphic (See Figure 21): In the last 140 years, since 1880, we have increased CO_2 by 38%, and that's that last graphic that we saw from the National Climate Assessment—I go back here a couple. So since 1880 here, we've gone up 38% in CO_2. We really have increased it. All right.

This graphic here is from Wismar, Germany. (**Figure 29**) Do you see any acceleration of sea-level rise as a result of that 38% increase? The acceleration due to that 38% is *zero*. Now why did I pick Wismar, Germany? Wismar sits on the Mecklenburg Bend, in the Baltic Sea. It is kind of like halfway between Norway and Sweden, and the Netherlands. Now Norway is rising, because the ice sheet, when it melted, took lots of

FIGURE 29

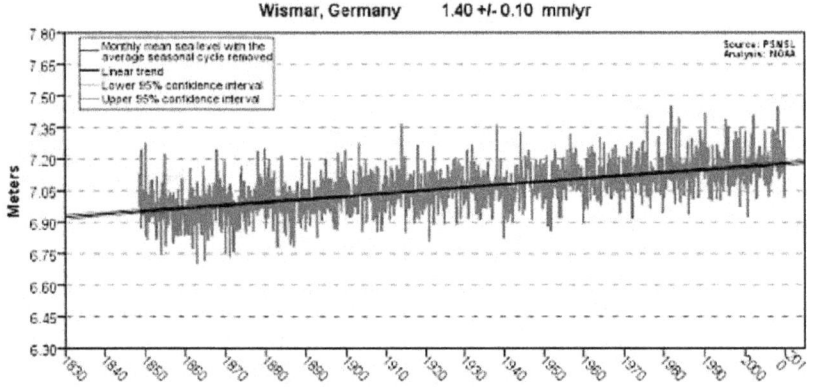

Massive 38% CO2 Increase Since 1880!

ANY sign of Sea-Level Rise Accelerating in Tectonically Inert Areas???

Wismar, Germany   1.40 +/- 0.10 mm/yr

weight off of Norway and Sweden, and Norway and Sweden are actually rising. So someone in Norway is saying, "Hey, sea levels are falling!" No, their land is actually going up. On the other side, you have Holland, and Belgium. Holland and Belgium, the land is sinking. It's like a see-saw. Norway goes up, Holland goes down. Wismar, Germany is in between the two of them: It is tectonically inert, it neither rises nor falls.

So a really good example of what real sea level rise is, and it's due mainly to oceanic warming. And it is straight and *totally unaffected* by the CO_2 that's coming into the air. Now if it is unaffected on the way up, that little minuscule reduction that we're talking about, the 400 million metric tons, is not even going to be *detectable*, in the *noise* of the sea level. The sea level is basically *unaffected* by CO_2.

If 38% increase can't make the sea level accelerate up, any *tiny* reduction that we make *cannot* affect it on the way down.

Electrify Africa!

So, that is my conclusion. Wish I could do more stuff for you guys.

So here's the final slide: "Can the Paris Proposals To Reduce CO_2 Have *Any* Effect on Sea-Level Rise?" (**Figure 30**) And the answer is: We don't even have an *instrument* that could measure it, on its effect on sea level—*it doesn't exist*. It's that inconsequential.

So why would you want to spend *billions* of dollars to reduce CO_2 by the 400 million metric tons, if you're not going to have any effect on sea level? What you could do with that money,—and here's where I am in league with these guys: What you could do with that money, is *electrify Africa*. Now what would happen if you electrify Africa? You would take people

FIGURE 30

Can Paris Proposals to Reduce CO2 Have ANY Effect on Sea-level Rise?

No Instrument Exists Today That Could Measure the Result!!!

who are sending their kids out, into the forest there to gather the firewood for four or five hours a day, so they can boil water in their huts, so they cannot get river blindness by drinking the water. And these people are spending their resources in that way. If we electrify Africa, those kids could be in school. They could be discovering cures for cancer. They could be doing *great things* for humanity!

And what we're doing is, we're saying, "We don't want more CO_2. We don't want more 'carbon pollution.'" It is a ruse, it is *fatal* for the world, because it will drive us back into the Stone Age, if it goes to its natural conclusion.

So if CO_2 is not affected by the oceans, the oceans have *no* change, don't spend the money trying to do that: Spend it where it counts.

I have one more thing. I'm part of the NASA TRCS Group; TRCS stands for "The Right Climate Stuff." We originated in Houston. We got together a couple years ago. We wrote a couple letters complaining to the administrator of the agency, that they were focusing on the wrong things, as you can see here.

We at the TRCS group want to make ourselves available, to any politician, any political party, and we will try to educate them on the real climate, and what's going on. This is not partisan: If a Democrat comes, or a Republican comes, they are going to get the same answers, because we're going to give them *data*, what you see there. And those facts are available, and you can contact either myself, tom@colderside.com or Hal-Doiron@yahoo.com. And the two of us will then redirect any questions to members of our group. We've got about 40 or 50 people now, who are in our group. It's a public service. We want to make sure you have the facts.

And those of you in the press here who want to follow me to Bulgaria, I'll be giving a much larger presentation with some of these slides, when I get to Bulgaria at the 10th Annual Water Conference; it's the last big water conference before Paris. And I hope that this message gets through to the people who are going to be going to Paris. And instead of spending $1,000 a night in hotel rooms and eating in the luxury restaurants, they could do something for the world, by diverting resources towards things like the electrification of Africa, and things like that. Thank you.

On Unity of Purpose, and On Christianity

Here are edited excerpts from Lyndon LaRouche's Fireside Chat of Thursday, Sept. 24, 2015.

On Unity of Purpose

Q: Hi, this is A— from New York, and hello everyone, and hi, Lyn. I spent a good portion,—during the time of the rally I was present and participating at the UN right there on First Avenue, this past Monday. And it was very similar numerically, from the signage standpoint, so the activity, the singing, the speeches, this was very similar in style and presentation to our earlier Wall Street rallies. And these have—by far, it seems to me—to have been the most effective. And this world stage of the UN was obviously a different backdrop, since largely, Wall Street now is kind of a tourist/ghost town combination. This was much more lively, I thought.

Yet, the process that all of us have been going through, as we continue to pay attention and work through some of the things that you work with us on, on Saturday, is becoming more and more evident to me. And it's very ironic to have fun at such a dangerous period. I've often seen organizers that are very strong doing that, over the years, and I would wonder, how that can actually be? I was there, but it was more out of duty, but not really engaging.

And perhaps this goes along with the type of resonance and harmony that you talk about, that is required, and I think—and not only myself, but I think this is happening throughout—while we're not large in number, the idea of having an effect on such a stage seems to me to be taking hold more and more; and at the same time, as you pointed out, never having the kind of fun where you're kidding yourself that, for example, Obama will capitulate and turn around and make a deal with Putin that he would keep.

So that the danger is as great as ever, yet I find it so ironic that when I left the rally to go back to work, I was very uplifted. So it's almost a strange thing—although I'm not complaining about it—that I find myself in this type of state, and it's a new experience for me.

I remember over years, sometimes listening in to some of the broadcasts you would do, where you were talking with members, and going through what the current situation was and what you were forecasting; and it was always very serious, with very serious consequences; then you would [talk] about what people needed to do, and I would really laugh hard, because at the end of the thing you would often say, "so let's have

EIRNS/Susan Bowen

LaRouche PAC activists rally in Times Square, New York Sept. 26

fun." And I would laugh and go, "What person could possibly have fun? [Given] everything you just said, I'm sitting here and I'm shaking in my boots."

Yet, that's what is happening now, at least for me. And I think I'm not special about this; I think it's happening with a lot of the other activists that are truly engaging. And, so I just think that's something I wanted to share with you and hear your thoughts on this process that we find ourselves in the middle of.

LaRouche: The problem is the relationship among people: When people are united in the sense that they have a conviction which they believe can be enforced for the good of mankind generally, then they're not divided, and therefore, they can come easily to cooperation; that is, real cooperation, where they're sharing experiences and find sharable experiences which mean something to them. In other words, what can you do for your children? What can you do for your neighbors? What can you do for other people around you?

The problem is that the system, the present U.S. system, generally divides people against one another; they don't have a sense of unity of purpose. Everyone has a different class: I'm of this class, he's of that class; he's got money, I don't have money; he's got opportunity, I don't have opportunity. Well, how do you get people together?

And the point is, we've come to a point of a great crisis, and every intelligent person, every intelligent adult knows that we're in trouble, and knows that we have to come together and create a unity of purpose. You know, stop this business about cheating on each other, that sort of thing. So therefore, the problem is, how can we steer ordinary people and sometimes extraordinary people, too, and how can we induce them to recognize that *their personal interest in life, depends on coming to a commonality of purpose for mankind as such*? And that's possible.

Just think about the ways, in just,—you go through walking around the street, and thinking about how many ways people are divided against each other. Now, there's some bad people out there, we all know that, right? You don't have to worry about that. But the ques-

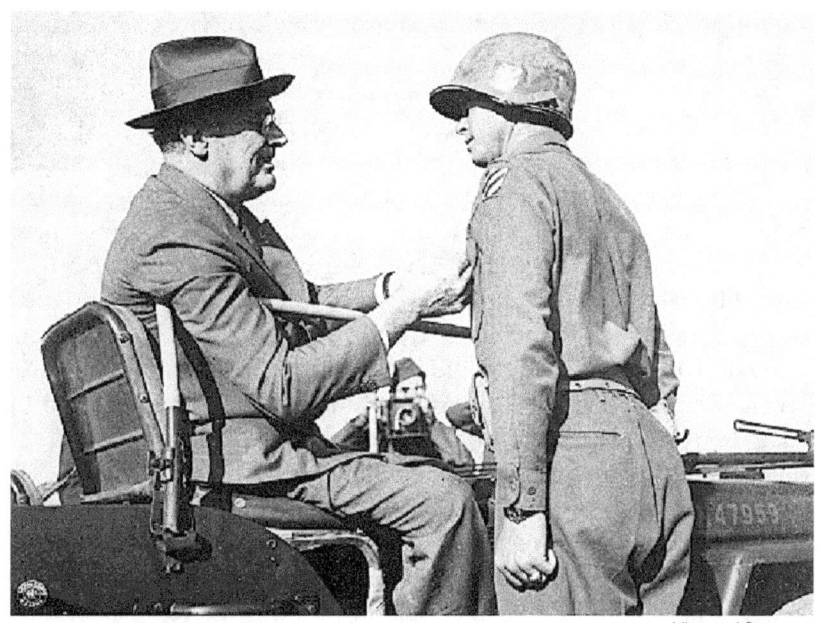
Library of Congress

America's unity of purpose around a world-historical mission was most dramatically evident in World War II. Here, America's leader in that war, President Franklin Roosevelt, is shown engaging with soldiers in Casablanca, Morocco in 1943.

tion is, you find that the ordinary people, you know, neighbors don't like each other; they're in the same kind of situation, they get in quarrels, they have competition, they try to cheat on each other to get a little advantage of this, or a perceived advantage.

And it's a division of mankind, a lack of a unity of purpose, a unity of mission, I think the time has come, right now in this great crisis, which of course is being celebrated in the Manhattan area in particular, that I think the time has come when we can think about pulling people together by talking to each other, and saying, "What kind of idiocy do we practice, when we quarrel with people we had no business quarreling with? Looking for quarrels, looking for advantages, trying to cheat, trying to get something from other people."

What you have to do is have this kind of commonality of purpose. And that's been lost. We used to have a great unity, in many periods like World War II we had a great unity among people who were sucked into World War II. And immediately after, once the Wall Street crowd and its crew influenced, you found that the people who had been united in defending the United States and other objectives during World War II, began to be *divided* against each other! As a matter of fact, the whole of the working population was divided! The families were divided!

And so, since that time, there has never been a consistent unity of effect, of loyalty to one another as people; it's always been played against them, Wall Street in particular played the population of the United States, against the population within itself!

What we have to do is realize we have a great crisis, a terrible crisis, globally as well as in the United States. And we have to recognize that we have to come to a unity of purpose, the way we did when we mobilized in World War II, recognize that! And we don't want to go back to World War II; I'm not suggesting that. But at a time when a people are united, about their commonality of their purpose,—we lost it so quickly; by the time we shut down the actual World War II, we began to lose the unity of the very people who had worked together to win World War II. And that's the kind of thing we've got to think about.

On Obama, and Again Unity

Q: Hi, this is K— F— from Massachusetts. Did we write on the website that Obama brought some nuclear missiles over to Germany?

LaRouche: Obama is in an operation: Obama intends, and is intended, to cause a general warfare which will decimate the population of the planet! That's what Obama is. And his stepfather had the same kind of position. This man is intrinsically evil. Everything he's done since he became President, has been evil. That is, everything I've known that he's done. And I got onto his tail early in the game, when he first made his real pitches around; and he immediately, quickly hated me. I think he still probably hates me beyond anything else, because he was *absolutely* unforgiving; he wanted to kill me.

So this guy, I know what he is. He is, as we say, "no damned good," and he shouldn't have been around anyway; he should have been off someplace. So that's the problem.

So the issue here is, how can we get the unity, effective unity of our own people, who recognize that they have certain intrinsic common interests. That doesn't mean they all agree with each other: It means that they have a sense, that they are members of the same species, rather than being enemies of their neighbors. If you've got a bad neighbor, you try to educate him; and if it's tough, why you can duck it a little bit and avoid the conflict.

But generally the point is, that society is *divided*; for example, the United States' society is divided! People are fearful of each other, they hate each other. Or they just resent each other, or they wish they could hate somebody.

This kind of thing, we've got to get an understanding, the meaning of,—as in warfare, as we did in World War II, you've got to recognize that the time comes, that you have a common interest. It doesn't mean you all agree on the same thing; it means that you realize that you, as a human being, have an interest in common, with a lot of other human beings in the same department.

What Is Creativity?

Q: Hi, good evening. This is T—, I'm calling from Virginia. I wanted to know more about creativity. Many people think they're creative and people often say, "I'm an artist, or I'm a musician, therefore I'm creative." But what defines creativity, and what method can be used to distinguish creativity from degeneracy? And more important, how can one access their own creativity? Thank you.

LaRouche: Creativity essentially is based on a principle which can be expressed most efficiently by saying that each person in life should, in the course of life, develop an ability to contribute progress to humanity around them. That's what the issue is.

The problem is, in the United States today, people sort of hate each other. Or they resent each other. They don't understand the point that mankind has to come to a certain commonality of objectives, and the object is the future of mankind as a whole. That is, not all the future and so forth, but the fact is that mankind must function in such a way as to benefit society, the living society as a whole; and the children of that society, and those who are dying or have just recently died, in the same period.

So you have to have a sense of what we call "solidarity"; say we call it a practical solidarity, rather than going to some rich kind of description, but just that: to recognize that your neighbors and so forth, are important to you, even if you don't like their tastes, if you don't like this or you don't like that about them—they don't wear the right clothes, they don't do this; but nonetheless, you've got to find a basis for solidarity with your neighbors, and your neighbors in the broader sense of the term.

Pope Francis and Hans-Joachim Schellnhuber

Q: Mr. LaRouche, this is K— in Silicon Valley, California. Thank you again for having these sessions, they're really awesome.

My question is, I understand that former [Archbishop of Boston, Cardinal] Sean O'Malley is pretty much Pope Francis's roommate, and my question is, do you feel that that may have had a significant influence on his political thinking, particularly in regard to global warming? O'Malley came from Boston.

LaRouche: Yes. I think that there are a lot of influences. For example, when you're talking about clergy, or the Catholic clergy in particular, and around people such as some of those in the Boston area who are relevant in this case, they're conflicted; because they've been told by Schellnhuber and other British agents, that this is the Pope's position, and I can't understand in any practical way, how the Pope could take that position that he has done, under Schellnhuber. Schellnhuber is obviously a very evil man; but on the other hand, you've got devout Catholics, in particular, who tend to be very devoted to the Catholic Church, and to what it represents for them. And therefore, when Schellnhuber, who is really a Satanic figure himself, intrinsically, gets in among them and gets a Pope to follow the Schellnhuber line, you say, what's happened? Has the Pope been taken over by the devil? By Satan?

And the point is, what we have to realize, if we want to be compassionate about this kind of disorder, you have to try to say, "we've got to rescue these guys." We've got to rescue them! And we've got to help them get free of Schellnhuber!

Look, you've got, in California, the current governor [Jerry Brown], and the guy is nuts! He's evil! He's actually evil!

And so, how do we get rid,—of when parts of the Catholic Church are recruited into supporting a Satanic policy, a literally Satanic policy! And they believe that the Papacy has laid out a demand that that policy be carried out! Which is what the case of the governor of California is: He's actually a Satanic figure in terms of his practice.

And so therefore, it's something we have to deal with. We can't just call names—and things, you've got to deal with this thing. You've got to try to rescue Catholics in particular, who get sucked into this thing. And say, "No, maybe the Pope said that, but that ain't right!"

That's the way you put it, because there is,—we

youtube

The professed atheist and Commander of the British Empire Hans-Joachim Schellnhuber was a leading presenter of Pope Francis's Encyclical Laudato Si'. *Here he is at the podium on June 29.*

know what the history of, for example, the Catholic Church is; we know what the history is. We know Nicholas of Cusa, for example. We know what Nicholas of Cusa represented, and still represents. We know other cases of the same nature. And you're going to say that Nicholas of Cusa is a fool? Well, that's pretty stupid, isn't it?

So therefore, if the Catholic Church is influenced by a Satanic figure such as Schellnhuber, and he *is* Satanic; if a Satanic figure like Schellnhuber takes over the Pope, you don't want to shoot the Pope! You don't want to quarrel with him. You want to treat him kindly, get him safely put away where he does not have any more of these evil kinds of impulses.

But the point is that Christianity does not belong to a Pope, in particular. It belongs to those who represent Christianity. And if somebody gets wild, like somebody becomes a cohort of Schellnhuber, and the Pope believes in supporting Schellnhuber's policy? You know, he's nuts! What do you do with a Pope who's a nut, or is mentally disturbed? What do you do? You get him gently put away and say, "Father, look you should take a little rest right now."

'I Was Thinking...'

Excerpts from Lyndon LaRouche's Dialogue with the Manhattan Project of September 26, 2105.

Q: Good afternoon, Lyn. This is B__ from New Jersey. We have now this ongoing process at the UN, which is, as many people have said (Helga particularly),—this is a turning point, or could easily be a turning point for the better. We're now seeing coming in to it a lot of motion going on, particularly with Europe breaking from Obama. I watched a press conference at the White House, in which some of the reporters were calling for the evaluation of how the books had been cooked on the so-called strategy against ISIS and other terrorism. And I think it's of particular importance that with the Syria thing, Obama's clearly worked himself out on a limb on this, and a lot of people want to take advantage of this. And my thinking, I think we're hearing a kind of sawing going on. And I'd like your thoughts on how we can coordinate that within the UN. What do we see going on, where we can get people joining in on a lot of that sawing?

LaRouche: Well, there are a number of ways you can deal with that. Just take one example. There's an institution called Wall Street. It's rather infamous or famous, as you may choose, but it's there. Now the fact about Wall Street is, Wall Street is dead; not dead in terms of moving, though there's some moving going on among shuffling of feet and so forth in the Wall Street area. But Wall Street has come to the terminal end of its own existence. It has come to that *now*.

What it's still pushing, trying to push some new imagination, some swindle,—they call it the "easing" policy. Wall Street says, "Easing, easing," which means cheating and stealing; and they keep doing that. Now we've reached the point where Wall Street can no longer

EIRNS/Dana Carsrud

LaRouche PAC organizers at an intersection near the United Nations, Sept. 28, 2105.

survive. And if we don't do something about it, if we operate within the acceptance of Wall Street's rule, then *we're* not going to survive.

The time has come to get Obama out of the White House entirely, immediately, and expose the fact that there is an absolute collapse of the presently existing economic system within the United States. What we can do is take from a map of Franklin Roosevelt, President Franklin Roosevelt. And Franklin Roosevelt introduced an institution and reforms which brought mankind into a higher state of existence, and he also eliminated what had been the earlier Wall Street system. When Franklin Roosevelt died, the first attempt by Truman and company, was to go back to the pre-Franklin Roosevelt system and to try to destroy everything that Franklin Roosevelt had represented. And it was the people *from* the Wall Street committee who did that. Truman was a traitor to the United States, in fact. That was his role.

FDR Library Photo collection

In his October 31, 1936 campaign speech at Madison Square Garden in New York City, FDR (on the left) delivered his famous line to Wall Street: "Never before in all our history have these forces been so united against one candidate as they stand today. They are unanimous in their hate for me—and I welcome their hatred."

1945: LaRouche's Mission Begins

So therefore, these are the issues which we have to take into account. We have to take into account the fact that we have had as the United States, as a people, we have had the resources in our hands,—if we had the will to use it,—to have saved the United States from all the horrors that have occurred since World War II. And I'm one of the survivors of World War II, not in an important way, but in the experience that I had, in terms of this thing. And I know what I saw.

I had an occasion when I was coming into India, I was landing in India. It was on the occasion of Franklin Roosevelt's death; and some fellow soldiers of mine came to me and said, "Can we talk to you in the evening?" And I understood what they were talking about. So we had a discussion, and I replied and said, "We've lived under a great President, Franklin Roosevelt. This is the thing for which we must fight. What he represented at the time of his death, is what he represented, and that's what *we* must represent." Now I tried a lot to get some of my fellow soldiers and others to mobilize on the basis of that position, that policy.

Many people, including great Presidents and great generals, agreed with what I was thinking, but they were defeated, often defeated. They became fewer and fewer, over the course of history. The number of people who were American officials, and so forth, talented people, who were actually competent has been reduced greatly.

If you want to find a good person to lead society in the United States, you have to find some of some very few people. Other people would like to do that, but they are denied the access to the means by which they could exert that kind of improvement. And therefore, from my standpoint, I say, "I am fighting, and others should be fighting to carry that position forth." We have to get Obama out of office quick, for the sake of the United States, but that's not where it starts. We have to continue that effort in order to make the United States *real* again, to itself.

Q: Hi, I'm E__ from Manhattan. I have a problem on deployment when I'm distributing literature, and informing people what we're thinking and trying to say. My favorite thing is usually to say, "Let's impeach Obama," but anyway, they go by, they don't stop, and they don't show any interest in anything. It's like they don't want to know. So I get so frustrated. Sometimes I curse them, or say things behind their back as they pass by.

What is your advice on how to get through to these people, who just don't seem to want to know anything?

LaRouche: Well, one thing I've been working on for some time is called Manhattan. It's always been that my experience was largely in Manhattan. I was recruited at the time of World War II. I was soon dragged into that. My experience was largely located in Manhattan. I then moved back into Manhattan at a later point. I had an important position as a consultant and so forth; and that got bounced by the FBI. I had a leading position, and so the FBI said, "We'll get you out of there. We want dumb people. We don't want smart people in our institutions."

So I've gone through that. And I understand these things fairly well, because I've had the opportunity to experience things in ways which are very useful to people, and which most people don't get a chance at. And they threw me in jail, and they did other things to me, but they didn't break me.

So the point is, we do have the ability now, because of the angry people in Manhattan. And also because of another factor. What do you think is going to happen to Wall Street? Wall Street is going to die! And all those buildings which are occupied by Wall Street and related interests, are going to suddenly go bankrupt. They're about to become bankrupt. Now what can we do? We can go back to Franklin Roosevelt's method, in dealing with a similar problem in the 1930s. And what he did, was shut down Wall Street.

Now what do you do when you shut down Wall Street? Well, Franklin Roosevelt knew what to do when you shut down Wall Street: You put in new institutions which are productive, instead of speculative. And he made a recovery of the United States, and made the United States again a great power under his prompting of influence. And people really swore by him, (not at him).

UN/Amanda Voisard

After Putin took on Obama in his UN speech, he joined the U.S. President in Obama's toast to the work of the United Nations, at a luncheon hosted by UN Secretary General Ban Ki-Moon.

And therefore, we've come to a time where we have to recognize, that all right, we've got a lousy President; the worst, most lousy President we've probably ever had! The most evil one! I can tell you, he's the most Satanic person ever in the government of the United States, the most *Satanic*.

Get Rid of Obama

And the only guy who compared was his stepfather, who was also *purely evil*. You have to know that Obama has a family record of being *pure evil*. He was less vigorous than his stepfather was, but he's just as *bad* as his stepfather, right now. He was the Satan of the occasion. And therefore, when we recognize that that's the thing that we have to get rid of: We have to get rid of Wall Street, which is another form of Satan's manifestations,—I guess its hooves, or something like that. But we must get rid of that thing, Wall Street!

We create the idea of a system of credit, as Franklin Roosevelt used the idea of a system of credit to reconstruct the economy and welfare of the American people. We have to do the same thing, the same practice again. When all those Wall Street towers collapse out of bankruptcy, we're going to have to have a Franklin Roosevelt or the likeness, take over those buildings, kick the scum out of the buildings, clean them up a little bit, and use them for more appropriate purposes.

Q: Good afternoon Mr. LaRouche, M__ from Queens. My question: We are the ordinary people, what can we expect from the UN General Assembly?

LaRouche: That's a big question, isn't it? Because we haven't got the answer yet, about what the result is going to be. Now, I would presume that the intention of President Putin of Russia, would be to do everything possible to get Obama in a tizzy. That is, it already has happened to a certain degree. Putin suddenly made a change, or what appeared to be a change in his policy. And suddenly, Obama freaked out! Because he thought he'd been swindled. He's enraged, absolutely enraged!

You have to know what Obama is: This man's stepfather was one of the biggest mass murderers in the southern waters, internationally; and the stepson followed his stepfather's training. The son was not quite as aggressive as the stepfather had been, but since recent times, Obama has become a true echo of his evil stepfather.

And therefore that's where the problem lies. We're going to have to get rid of what Obama represents. Now, it's very easy to do, in law, because he deserves to be thrown out of office, and there are many reasons for throwing him out of office. There are more opportunities to throw him out of office than he has lives. So therefore, get rid of this guy, dump him!

He was a British creation, anyway. Obama was part of this Asia operation; his stepfather was his master.

He's a true copy of his stepfather, who was an evil man, a mass murderer, and a very evil man, and he has the same characteristics, still today. Just think of the number of people that Obama has killed: People on the record, who were arbitrarily killed by the order of Obama. Not because they were guilty of anything, not because there were actual changes against them. But Obama wanted to kill them. He killed little boys; he killed young people generally. He kills, kills, kills, kills!

He terrifies the people inside his own administration; he's a tyrant. He's a man of intrinsic evil. If we can remove this President from his office, I guarantee you that the future of mankind will be greatly improved, relatively speaking.

kremlin.ru

Building bridges: Russian President Putin speaks with German Chancellor Angela Merkel on May 10, at the conclusion of celebrations of the 70th anniversary of the end of World War II in Europe.

Q: Hi, Lyn. My name is A__. I just had a general question on going into the next week, in organizing in the UN, because we are coming across a lot of diplomats, a lot of organizations affiliated with the UN, that are really interested in our initiative,—you know, the U.S. joining the BRICS, let alone their countries [joining BRICS]. And it's interesting, just the previous question, it is the case a lot of these countries that do come over to our table, they're not part of the BRICS; they're Third World nations, but they're very interested in our initiative. But, it's like a general question: How can we escalate the next coming week, in organizing these people in the UN?

Terrified People

LaRouche: Well, you're going to get an answer to that, in a sense, by the headlong conflict between Obama and Putin. And China is also involved in this already. Other people, other nations are also involved in this issue right now. So this is not an isolated case.

The point is, getting Obama thrown out of office, is the most essential thing that could be done, now, by anybody anywhere. Get rid of this guy. The next thing, we get rid of the Saudi empire. And once you've got Obama thrown out, then you go out and you close down that empire, the Saudi empire, which is one of the worst afflictions of the planet. But Obama is worse. So we get Obama out of the way first, and then we go and clean up Saudi Arabia. And then we can clean up some other things after that.

But the people of the United States and the world in general, are terrified people by and large. They are not warriors. They may have equipment of warfare, but they're not warriors by instinct, and therefore you have to do some coaching, to muster people into doing what has to be done for mankind.

And what happens? Everybody looks right now at the world, for example, at Putin. "Ah! There's Putin! Ah, he's a courageous guy! He's going to take this on, he's going to take that on; he's the guy to go to." He's the guy who went to some of the issues there, and so he's considered the guy to go to. And other people say, "Oh, yes, we're also involved in this, we're very much supportive of this thing." And so you have a great number of people and nations who are willing to stand by and say, "Oh yeah, I'm all for Putin." [laughter] But, who's going to support him? Who's going to deliver the goods, shall we say? And that's the problem.

But my view is, in my experience, if you—as we're already doing—you have to look at the change that occurred within the nations of Europe, since recently. Everybody had been hating Putin, officially; nations across the trans-Atlantic region, had been *hating Putin*! Then, suddenly one day, the ruling forces in Germany said, "Oh, no! this guy is very useful. He's saving people's lives; he's intervening to defend people's lives. Oh, he's a good guy!" And that's the way it works!

So what happens is, somebody does something, an act of courage, and somebody else says, "Oh! Now I see what you meant!" And that's the way you have to look at it. People are not intrinsically courageous; and they are hesitant. They don't like to be courageous. But anyone who's gone through war,—you know, actual war,—knows what this is like, what war is like. War is scary!

I was never in much danger in my military service; it was very limited. I was assigned to my duties and I performed my duties in various parts of the world. But most people don't have the guts to win wars; and if they do it, they often do it with great stress on their nerves. So don't demand too much of people. If you can push people into recognizing that perhaps they could survive, against something which they know to be evil, they may, with some hesitation, actually mobilize themselves to change the way things are going.

Q: Thank you for taking my question. My name is M__, and I'd like to ask you—you may have answered this already, about two people before; but eventually Russia seems destined to be the main link in Eurasia politically and economically. They're already there geographically. But all the things that have happened in the past week, in Vladivostok, and the parade in China, and also Merkel agreeing to stop being an echo chamber for the West there about her agreement about Assad being put in. Do you see any other European power that might eventually leave the NATO pact, at least verbally and sort of come behind Putin, and any other shift that you see there?

LaRouche: Well, there are two things that can be said about that, on that subject. First of all, that Putin is a unique figure. Now I've had a lot of activity with people, in post-Soviet system operations with Russia. In other words, I was not part of the old system, the old Russian system; but I was part of the new system, what was left over from the older one. And I was associated with a group of people in Russia who came to me and asked for me to make my contributions to policymaking, for Russia to get out of the mess it had been dumped into. The whole Soviet system had collapsed, it disintegrated, gone! So there were some people who were trying to deal with that problem, that ménage.

And I was brought into this, to visit Russia; I was invited by some Russians to do that. I conducted a lot of interventions at various points in Russia, and the last contact I really had of any significance in causing Russian policy was when Putin, at the same time that I was operating on this thing, had started his big campaign to free Russia of the conditions of Russia at that time. And that has been a relatively long period of time.

Who is Vladimir Putin?

So there have been ups and downs. In the meantime, I've had very little contact with Russia in general, because of my own health conditions and so forth. But in terms of principle, Putin has recreated Russia. I don't want to make that a statement of exaggeration; it's simply that he was the guy, who as a leader within Russia under those conditions, dealing with a particular problem, has persisted in defending Russia, with increasing effectiveness over that period of time, and has also made contributions to other nations, cooperation with other nations, and the programs to try to defend nations against certain problems.

So that's the way you have to look at it. This is not a streak of genius in itself: Putin has really worked over a period of his lifetime, since I knew what his operation was; since I began to know his operation. And now it's at that stage where he's now become that absolutely indispensable factor, in Europe and the trans-Atlantic region particularly, to get the world out of this mess. And you see that, you see what the operation is; you see the changes: Germany, France, for example; the importance of China, the importance of India. All these things are part of this great movement which is centered on Putin.

Now, he's not just some great genius in the ordinary sense of that remarkable case. He's a practical man, an impassioned man, and one who remembers deeply that many members of his family died in defending the very lives of their family in Leningrad, now called St. Petersburg, in the old Soviet Union. And that legacy has been picked up, finally, by Putin. And Putin has been the one person from Russia, who in the course of the development of his own career has built Russia into a force, tied to China, tied to India, tied to other parts of the planet, and they're doing good. They're doing Russian good; it's Russian-style, Russian good. And that's there!

Right now, Putin is the most important figure in ensuring the *possibility* that Obama will be thrown out of office. Because if Obama is *not* thrown out of office,— and you know his history and his stepfather's history before then. What's happened now, what Putin has done with these current events in Manhattan now, *may have saved civilization*. If Putin is successful against Obama, that may be the salvation of civilization; not because he's a great warrior, but because his role, at a crucial point, is that important.

EIR Silk Road Report in Chinese Presented in Beijing

by William C. Jones

Sept. 29—At a press conference today in Beijing, sponsored by *EIR* and the Chongyang Institute for Financial Studies, Helga Zepp-LaRouche, the initiator of the Schiller Institutes, and William Jones, the Washington Bureau Chief of *Executive Intelligence Review*, keynoted the presentation of the Chinese translation of *EIR*'s groundbreaking report, "The New Silk Road Becomes the World Land-Bridge," to the public.

There were around 70 people in attendance, including 15 representatives from the Chinese media, as well as a few officials from government entities and numerous think-tanks. In addition, nine leading Chinese scholars made comments about the report and its significance for the Chinese "One Belt, One Road" project. The Chongyang Institute has also agreed to be a co-sponsor of the report.

Helga Zepp-LaRouche outlined the work of the Schiller Institute in developing the Silk Road/World Land-Bridge project for over 20 years, outlining the efforts that went on for decades to realize the report. Its circulation represents a unique opportunity for changing the course of history, she said. "We must get away from geopolitics and move to a new paradigm for mankind," Zepp-LaRouche said.

The comments from the scholars were absolutely effusive about the report. One scholar said that he had known the Schiller Institute for a long time and had learned much from its ideas. "They have very special ideas about the economy, emphasizing the notion of physical economy. Lyndon LaRouche developed the notion of negentropy to explain the laws of economics.

William C. Jones

This is the poster which the Chongyang Institute for Financial Studies put out to advertise the Beijing press conference on the release of EIR's Silk Road report in Chinese. It lists the scheduled speakers.

We cannot allow capital to control everything. We must control capital," he said.

Another scholar noted that the Schiller Institute had a different view of the economy from most economists in emphasizing the underlying importance of infrastructure. "Mrs. LaRouche has made great progress with her ideas," he said. One scholar noted that China's "One Belt, One Road" policy represents the beginning of a new world order, and that we must find out how it differs from the world order led by the United States. One scholar from the Chinese planning agency underlined the uniqueness of the report, praising the work behind it and urging Chinese experts to take heed of the methods of analysis used in the *EIR* report.

Again, another scholar who had just finished reading the Chinese report the evening before, said that it had obviously been written with a global perspective, noting that it is about forecasting the future, rather than simply explaining the past.

There was a lively question and answer period, and many people came up to get their copies signed by the authors. The Chongyang Institute has already purchased 1,000 copies of the report for distribution to its networks and to scholars in China.

EIR's English-language report was released in November of 2014. The 400+ page report includes an extensive section on the Metrics of Progress, as developed by economist Lyndon LaRouche, as well as extensive expositions of how the New Silk Road development can uplift the economies of every section of the world economy. More information is available at http://world-landbridge.com/